George Lansing Raymond

Life Below

In Seven Poems

George Lansing Raymond

Life Below
In Seven Poems

ISBN/EAN: 9783744704533

Printed in Europe, USA, Canada, Australia, Japan

Cover: Foto ©Thomas Meinert / pixelio.de

More available books at **www.hansebooks.com**

LIFE BELOW:

IN SEVEN POEMS.

NEW YORK:
PUBLISHED BY HURD AND HOUGHTON.
Cambridge: Riverside Press.
1868.

Entered according to Act of Congress, in the year 1868, by
HURD AND HOUGHTON,
in the Clerk's Office of the District Court for the Southern District of New York.

To
HIS PARENTS,

WHOSE GENEROUS CONFIDENCE HAS ALLOWED THE AUTHOR

MEANS TO CULTIVATE AND TIME TO RIPEN

These first fruits of Art,

THEY ARE MOST AFFECTIONATELY

DEDICATED.

CONTENTS.

	PAGE
THE SCALE: DO	1
CHOOSING	5
RE	45
DARING	47
MI	85
DOUBTING	87
FA	121
LEARNING	123
SOL	161
LOVING	163
LA	199
SERVING	201
SI	247
WATCHING	249
DO	285

LIFE BELOW.

THE SCALE;

DO.

"I PURPOSED to relate some tales of life
Which yet should be the tales of more than one,
For they should be of soul-life, not of sense.
Our deeds extern are transient. There is life,
More than what smiles at home, and bends at church,
And bows upon the street; beneath things seen,
Their unseen, constant, universal cause,
The life, which good men hope shall be eternal.
Express'd in act, forever flexible
To circumstance, it still is lord of forms.
As child, it starts to gain its choice: opposed,
Retires; then, planning wiser ways, anon
It starts to do, anon shrinks back to think,
Till alternating strife be call'd to rest
With that Eternal Cause who thus allow'd
Experience to apprehend and aid
The onward course of universal gain.
Of such life did I purpose to relate,
Not all unmoved by consciousness of power,
Relying still upon that Source which gave,
And shall give greater, strength to all who strive
With what they have." So spake the man of books,
The village author, 'mid a little throng,
At sunset gather'd, ere dispersing home,

To chat of news, around the blazing hearth
That warm'd a small town's post-office and store.
"Alas," he added then, "this ruthless war!
You know my scribe went last week, and that scribe
Was versed in all notes of my earlier life
From which I'd thought to frame these later tales.
I could not keep him back, had gone myself
But for this palsied hand; and, yet, 'twas hard!
No healthy hand to loan in all the town —
My work, you see, like yours, must wait for peace."
"No!" said the young store-clerk, "there I protest:
The business hours aside, this hand is yours."
The words call'd forth his master: "Not too fast!
From dawn to dark 's enough for your slight frame;
That too with double work already, boy." —
And thence a brisk discussion sprang apace,
Till, in the end, each of the company
Had vouch'd himself best fitted for a scribe.

The old man smiled; nor would accept, at first;
But last he said to waxing earnestness:
"This war, at least, shall yield to compromise!
My tales begin with youth, and end with age;
Haply, if my scribes fit these spheres of thought
They'll aid the younger, and the older too.
Let me select, according, then, to years;
And choose the boy first!" So it was agreed:
And furthermore; that each, when he had written,
Should read his part before a social club
Form'd of those present and their families.

Some time had pass'd; and then the young store-clerk
Seem'd taught in riddles, and in strange conceits;
And had grown well-nigh famous in the town.
To those well versed his self-vague talk appear'd
Like one's who'd rummaged not digesting parts
Of rat-gnaw'd libraries. In after time,
More wisely could the wise surmise its source.

INTRODUCTION.

For he had raved of mystic numbers, thus:
"Like to the seven days that mark the week,
Of scales, men trace in music, stars and plants,
And dream in heavens, hells, and worlds; as tho'
Nature herself had tallied what she'd made;
Seven stratas counting through the senseless rock,
Seven forms in life, as many in each form,
The last one man, in Nature's Sabbath-time,
Living, perchance, seven spheres of history —
All men, and each!" — and one old carper 'd told:
"As tho' a rock and spirit were alike;"
How "he'd said: 'man and nature had one life!
Augustine, Plato, and Pythagoras,
Had they not deem'd the soul a number? sphere? —
Tho' yet, who were full wise enough to read
Down underneath rough angles and rude lines
To methods mathematical, that speak,
Like children's faces of the soul beneath,
Deep traits of this divine philosophy?'"
Thus did the youth pass for a clever lad,
To make the girls laugh, and to bluff the boys,
Long ere the evening came when his proud mother
His neck-tie pinn'd, and kiss'd his cheek, and said:
"Now dear, and don't forget — read loud enough!"

POEM FIRST.

CHOOSING.

I.

LIFE hangs poised on slender moments; all
    Eternity on Time;
And the still small voice betokens presence of a
    sway sublime.
Tread, as light as dreams, may wake the soul's
    hush'd spontaneity,
Rouse the source whence Thought and Action issue
    toward their destiny, —
Toward the good, if moved by footsteps echoed
    from a path of weal;
Toward the ill, if slyly summon'd by the craft of
    baser zeal.
It may be a sound, a fragrance, or a light, glides
    near the mind;
Something stirs a wish within us; something gleams,
    we glance to find;
And we start; and then press forward, past op-
    posing scenes of youth;
Past all life, perchance, till Old Age falls to spring
    the gates of Truth.

II.

Everything, in art or nature, robed in rich or rude attire,
Gathers beauty by possessing power to prompt some pure desire.
For the Will commands her own charms; and, from wide-distracted throne,
Waives all claim of rival suitors for a pure Desire alone.
Thus, we find, a fairer fancy blooms in dear but distant views,
Through which blind or banish'd poets search a dream of halo hues.
Thus, we find, when Evening Shadows bend about the couch of Day,
Life, array'd in fresh attraction, lies along the growing gray.
For the dim relief of objects woos our Wonder and Surmise,
And the Sibyl Stars invite to solve the tale of silent Skies;
While the zest of Aspiration, as more sovereign plans evolve,
Crowns the brow of meek Conjecture with the flush of bold resolve.

III.

Is it strange if, such an evening, through the smouldering lines of strife,
Such an evening, far and hazy, loom the sweetest scene of life?

Is it strange if Memory, gazing through a wake of
    stormy skies ;
Or an older Mind recall it, clad in graver, wiser
    guise ?

IV.

Sunset waned ; and I sat watching, with sensations
    strange and wild,
Till I grew a thing mysterious, and too grand to
    be a child.
I was not of earth, or heaven, but was one with
    that mild light,
Which had veil'd in awe the hills before the sacred
    steps of Night ;
And, through all the clouds that floated, rose the
    forms of angels fair ;
And I seem'd to feel their whisper in the warm
    breath of the air.
Far adown the west I traced them, till their min-
    gling lines were brought
Nigh a boundless mountain, gleaming o'er a peace-
    ful sea, I thought ;
Where anon were purple islands, lax in languid
    Autumn-noon ;
And, a-sail the azure distance, came in view the
    crescent moon.
On her stilly course I linger'd, till, with joy and
    marvel great,
I descried a wondrous city, glimmering past a
    golden gate !

V.

Ah, it was a wondrous city, that bright city in the cloud!
How its towers and turrets glisten'd, with what wealth of light endow'd!
How the walls which coil'd around it glow'd adown their winding belt!
And how flash'd the dancing crystals, which about the bulwarks dwelt!
Underneath that sight, triumphant, stretch'd a tempest black along;
'Twas a diapason, rolling, rich but rough, below a song!
For, above, in countless number, press'd the domes, and pierced the spires, —
Domes, more pure than pearly altars, sanctified by Heaven-lit fires!
Domes, of form to rival dreaming! domes, of every higher hue!
Join'd with spires from darkness pushing, till the peaks effulgence knew!
Spires, like prayers, from vapors struggling, gaining glory round the Bar!
Spires, like Hope, to falter never, till it touch the fated star!
Then, deep down — my gaze profaning — what retreats for bliss I found,
'Mid the weird-illumined mansions, and the peerless streets around!
Streets, as shafts of light, far shooting, dying like the sun from view,

Through a shade of forests, brilliant still by radiant
    fruit that grew!
Beauteous city! how I loved it! how forgot this
    present star!
There content, like him of Pisgah, with the prom-
    ise, tho' so far!

VI.

When, at length, to self returning, my Desires grew
    mutinous;
And too rebel Meditation to their tocsin murmur'd
    thus:
"Six years; it is long to languish, with no teacher
    but my God,
In these stolen hours of study, snatch'd from swine,
    and sweat, and sod.
Wherefore was I left an orphan, and a ward, with-
    out a joy,
To that sateless judge? His Satan seem'd a better
    breed of boy!
I suppose — a frame so feeble — he had hopes that
    it would die;
And so bound me out as plowboy, to make friend-
    ship with the sky!
Bound to those with mood repulsive; finding water
    for the fire;
Yes, a hiss for every spark that holds a glimmer-
    ing of desire!
Heaven above: one thing I pray for; not release
    from toil and pain;
But the work that meets both cheerly, facing still
    a chance for gain.

Lead me toward those waiting regions, thick with
  thought, by man unknown,
Filling space, from orb and orbit, through to glory
  round the Throne;
Lead me up, that I may find there, light which
  has not been possess'd;
Light, to guide Earth's wavering Faith! a cynosure
  of certain rest!

VII.

"Vain, oh, vain, this hope. Its cheer is hollow, as
  were demon's mirth.
This is weak — to sigh for Heaven when one's
  made to scrape the Earth!
Better far to keep the level; turn from hights
  suggesting lore; —
Wisdom makes the vulgar worthless; — herd with
  brutes here, evermore!
Shall I? Ears, no lie can lull you to that distant,
  holy strain!
Eyes, no lower gloss can dim you to the stars
  which o'er you reign!
Toil-worn Hands, right dainty fingers serve a soul
  less coarse than we!
Thorny Ways, the Palace carpet hugs no richer
  blood than ye!
Storms that rage, your rivals gather here beneath
  as restless brows!
And their thunders crave report from something
  else than grating plows!

VIII.

"Oh, how oft, when I've been lying underneath
    the great oak-trees,
Or mysterious stars of midnight, I have dream'd
    of endless ease!
And of that, divine, had visions, fill'd for compre-
    hension vast,
So that mine, with utmost effort, caught but por-
    tions, as they pass'd;
Portions yet of charm so potent, that, renewing
    every main,
Thought would still soar on to match them, and
    would soar, and soar in vain,
Till, to its bewilder'd yearning, all things mixt, to
    merge in shade,
Through which sank the train of grandeur, and the
    hope which found it fade.
Woe of mortals; to be grounded, 'mid the mists
    of one small sphere,
While bright beacons, from high havens, throng the
    midnight, far and near!
Oh but soul! in sight of Heaven, favoring winds
    cannot forsake!
Life — it moves, in tardy progress, tho' so slowly
    grow its wake.
Onward! Oft some keener thinker, pressing through
    a myth, long sought,
There reveals the flags of wisdom far along the line
    of thought!"

IX.

With emotions, ne'er allaying, I remain'd ; and watch'd that cloud,
Till those living forms seem'd buried in a gently gather'd shroud.
Yet, my gaze still rested on it: naught! oh! naught of good can die!
But, for changeful resurrection, sinks to rise, and purify!
Blessings grieve us, when they leave us ; but they leave no sunless gloom :
Springs a new life of reflection: and more beauteous thought to bloom.
While enwrapt in contemplation, lo! came suddenly a change!
All the width of western heaven drew apart, with flashing strange!
Whence pure Clouds in speed assembled, as if, thus, to screen from me
Tens of thousand flames, which lit a passage — through Infinity!
Rapture then my brain bewilder'd! Every thought to passion flew!
"Surely! surely! Celebration Brightness crowns with halo new!
It may be an angel greeting to some saint!"— Then, lost in flight,
Flits this whim, where lights another! for behold! a stranger sight!
Swift, from flash to flash augmenting, as a torrent seeks the sea.

Streams that fire from out the distance, surging,
    surging nearer me!
Now, 'twas my whole spirit flutter'd. "Here's the
    World's last ransom brought!
Crampt! how crampt these fleshly fetters! Yes,
    they burst! they burst! I thought.
Near such end, the wish grew gentler, satisfied to
    wait a time;
Satisfied; for that, which lured it, sent before a
    soothing chime.
Sweet it was, with deeper sweetness, than our mor-
    tal breathing brings;
Speaking peace, profound and lasting, as the love,
    from which peace springs;
Full subduing all the being, in a spell, resistless
    found
As the wreck'd and sinking sailor feeling silence
    steal around;
Nor can memory retain it; better bid yon meadow
    nook
Hold the whole .great rain, which blest it, on its
    journey down the brook.

X.

Ay! when men, who speak, directing toward a
    spring of healing truth,
Toward a stimulant of beauty, pure to stay an
    endless youth,
While attempting, falter, blunder, and, with sense
    dividing wide,
Void of close and clear expression, end where
    almost all deride,

Blame them not! the case is human! words with
  ease bear thoughts below,
But they fail beneath the press of higher themes,
  which overflow!
Many guiding views beyond us loom but dimly
  understood :
Many schemes are hatch'd to famish where our im-
  perfections brood.
Oh! how oft, e'en stirr'd to rescue dearest friend
  from threaten'd woe,
Or to point him toward successes, we have yearn'd
  that wish to show;
When the lack of tact or temper has equipt advice
  amiss,
Frail as Truth that leans and whispers hob-and-
  nob with Prejudice.
And how often, as the sunshine, or the lightning
  blazed within,
We would save a gleam of duty for the virtue of
  our kin,
When, if brighter could reflect it, we, at least, were
  dull as night,
Striving ever, failing ever, half our view to mirror
  right!
Foremost of Endowments precious! Faith fails
  not, that can but feel!
Yet for Faith, how blest the mission, that can, too,
  the near reveal!
Station'd where, 'mid doubt and darkness, Thought,
  which moves through mystery,
Longs to point to things alluring, longs to spy,
  what others see,

There, with gifts from Heaven enkindled, flashing
    light to Teaching's aid,
And, for anxious Quest, disclosing Truth that lives
    beyond the shade!

XI.

This for preface: That remember'd sòmehow thus,
    in measures, ran:
Varied aye to changeful music, not restricted by
    the plan:
But each single voice swell'd freest; either past all
    discord sweet;
Or with depth, below disturbing, tuned to harmony
    complete.
Thus the words: and seem'd to purport praise to
    One of Sovereign Might,
Recognized by eager senses as the Royal Source
    of Light:

XII.

"Hail! hail! hail!
    Eternal Glory, hail!
Ye powers of right, attend the Light,
    With praise for every ray!
All, all were blight, and no delight,
    Without that blissful sway!
Before 'd begun a star or sun,
    High Splendor fill'd the Throne,
When, ere the birth of air or earth,
    Jehovah lived alone.
Gleam! gleam! gleam!
    And ever brighter beam!
Far, far away, through endless day,
    Invoke the growing theme!

"Hail! hail! hail!
　　Infinite Goodness, hail!
From Heavenly hight, through day, through night,
　　Down, down to deepest Hell;
From central Throne to vacant zone,
　　Thy radiant Mandates dwell.
Move forth in might, where all is bright!
　　And cheer, where sometimes shade!
In weeping sphere, the rainbow rear!
　　Then, pierce to darker glade!
　　Shine! shine! shine!
　　The universe is thine!
Through blackest Hell, burst, full and fell,
　　Like lightning, flame divine!

"Hail! hail! hail!
　　Almighty Power, hail!
At thy command, 'mid blazing grand,
　　The holy army hies;
With flash of worth about the earth,
　　Pursuing lust and lies.
Through wind, and wave, and crystal cave,
　　They charge, in far control;
And, marshall'd round, with thunder sound,
　　The Tempest tongues enroll.
　　Wail! wail! wail!
　　Ye powers of darkness quail!
No respite till the Wrong is still,
　　And Foulness found — to fail!

"Hail! hail! hail!
　　Unchanging Promise, hail!
O'er storms and jars, the flickering stars
　　Burn on, our long fear through.
Aurora lights her giddy hights.
　　The comet cleaves the blue.
On sand and sea the Shadows flee.
　　Awaking winks the Dew.

The morn is nigh. The breeze is high.
   Far break thé Fogs anew!
   Speed! speed! speed!
   And gild the gloomy mead!
Through every clime call up the prime
   Of holy Creed and Deed!"

XIII.

Ere the Echoes, far excited, learn'd the tones of half the lay,
I descried the choir that chanted, treading down their starry way: —
Such a sight, as all have witness'd, roused by Morn's first Herald-Gleam,
Floating up the edge of slumber, in a just awaking dream —
Angel forms, no man could number, stretching onward through the light,
Round a chariot, framed of splendor, drawn by steeds of wavering white,
Soft of step, which skipt the vapors; and with wings of texture rare,
Whence there throbb'd a murmur'd music, as they lightly struck the air.
In the chariot sat a Being, fair, beyond the reach of rhyme,
Fledged for dauntless flight of fancy, to recall the mien sublime.

XIV.

While I kneel'd, entranced, she reach'd me, then, as angel bands disperse,

With a low command, so love-full it could lull the universe,
"Come," said she, "and sit beside me." And I rose, I wis not how,
And within the place was seated. I had not known bliss till now!
'Thwart the earth, and through the vapors, over land and lake it springs,
With a swift but gentle motion, marshall'd on by beating wings;
Till, through long horizons pulsing, flash'd and pass'd us beacon gleams,
And uncertain forms of twilight, floating storm-toss'd lightning streams.

XV.

Then, full much, I long'd to ask her, where we were, how far my home;
But while yet I dared not, kindly, knowing whither thought did roam,
She replied: "My child, that homestead, it is fixt within a star!
We have left the bounds of matter, here is burst each prison bar,
Out from which, with straiten'd senses, and a saddening sway of strife,
Souls, like convicts, through their grating, steal a luring glimpse of life.
Here are regions, where the spirit, freed from fettering time and space,
Wings her flight through scenes eternal; reading thought as face reads face;

Gaining wisdom from the wise, who wonder with sincerity,
Pure, beyond the darkening mien that decks an ill supremacy.
In the world, brains mould to bodies, but across the border line,
Royal minds must share their purple: slaves with kings become divine.

XVI.

"Oh! if but one spirit vision flared to reach the groping man,
In one glance were comprehended more than life-long search can scan! —
Soft, my steeds. — The stars are slumbering. There are dreams afloat to-night.
Gaze, and gain, while passing through them, segments of angelic sight!
Circle these with all bright fancies, forged in all these burning spheres,
From Arcturus, past Orion, far as where the Cross uprears;
Conjure clear as minds that muse them, diverse as their interest;
Add completed recollection; and all thoughts that each suggest;
Then, conceive a saint's possession thus matured from hight to hight,
Naught too full for God to render from resources infinite!"

XVII.

As she spoke, along the gloaming, there appear'd what seem'd a grove,
Shading maddest mixtures, thronging back through labyrinths unwove!
Fountains, arbors, caves and mountains, wolds and wildernesses grand,
Hung to wild fantastic fortunes o'er a dizzy dearth of land;
Based on clouds, all diamond-dappled, emerald meads and mottled meres,
Spann'd by bounding balustrades, which mesh'd the loops of spray-shot piers;
Trees, heaven-high, where swung blithe moonbeams rock'd as on Behemoth's bed;
Velvet fields, with tender grasses humbled 'neath a fairy's tread;
Flowers and fruit, which flush'd and nodded where alternate Autumn-sheen,
Like a flood of amber, whelm'd thick twilight-tangled evergreen;
Houses, gardens, tombs and temples, flags and fleets, and, round them swept,
Masses, mazes of inventions, every whim, e'er wrought or wept;
Birds and beasts, all shapes, all sizes, dancing, dozing, clamoring, shy,
Strown, as if on waves of vapors, shored afar in searchless sky!

XVIII.

Soon she named, about the forest, forms: — some boldly faced, some fled —
Snow-white Nixies, with pink Pixies, pilfer'd from lone baby bed:
Jinn and Shedeem, mask'd and capering, wild as clowns in circus rings:
Peris, giddy with full fragrance, flirting down on dove-like wings:
Then, below them, Neck and Kelpie, match'd to deluge plump Storm-Karl:
Drakes, a-see-saw rill-rockt lilies, dodging from the Merman's snarl:
Drunk Leprechaun, dash'd for brogue, and tussling with each huger swell,
As he split the laughing waters in a love-warpt fairy-bell:
On the ledges Dwarfs a-droning, and, seduced from secret cave,
Duergar, the little scamp, with mien as scrimpt as gold he gave!
Deevs, beneath thick horns and eyebrows, envying Korred's shaggy head:
Ruths, and Throlls, and Trows, in gray green, tossing pigmy caps of red:
Greeting shrunken sly Hobgoblins, hitch'd to half the cellar's ware:
Danish Nis, and Gallic Latin, all of Bedlam crowding there:
Brownie, brave by plaid and thistle! Cobalt, blooming big with beer!

Braggart snobs, astride a lion — whelp, you'd know,
    of some new peer !
And the Elves, like wintry smoke, a-wheel to Hog-
    folk's low refrain ;
Or, detected, swiftly skulking toward the bolstering
    leaves amain !

XIX.

But I turn'd to stranger marvel : — just beyond my
    finger's end,
Lilted near the weest wonder that could bid the
    eyelids bend !
One might deem it a stray snow-flake, sliding down
    the thin star-rays :
Truth reveal'd a cunning chariot, fill'd with cheery
    little fays ;
And up through the shifting atoms of the air that
    lay between
Oozed a tiny ditty, tuning from within its sheeny
    screen.

XX.

"To-night, to-night, my fairies white,
  We'll rig a jolly spree !
But first a tune to tease the Moon —
  She's pointing there you see !
Ho ! ho ! who'd own that dewy throne,
  Or tent the spider weaves ?
Ho ! ho ! who'd go where roses grow,
  Or romp the springy leaves ?
Her tinsel Tags may flirt and play,
  Till all the calyx crush away !
    Who cares ? — I dont ! — Do you ?

"But there's a maid whom Love has laid —
  Ha! ha! a dainty bit! —
Aboard a dream, with brain a-scream!
  Queen Mab's a wicked wit!
Come! come! a jump! and land a-thump!
  To dance about her heart!
'Twill beat and beat; ha! ha! how sweet!
  My soles are all a-smart!
We'll tickle her neck, and tickle her toes,
And tickle her little lips under her nose! —
  Who cares? — I don't! — Do you?

"That mourner grim, we'll bother him.
  He tugs too stiff a brow!
We'll whiz and whiz about his phiz,
  And twit the mouth, I vow:
Then hide and seek in hair so sleek,
  And down the wrinkles spare;
And ply his eye, if dry, too dry,
  And slide the lashes there;
And when big drops begin to flow,
How we will dodge the flood, oh ho!
  Who cares? — I don't! — Do you?

"Hurrah! for peep of Earth asleep!
  We'll twist things, ere we're flown!
The sire shall be a baby wee:
  The lass a lad alone:
The parson mad: the plagued a-glad:
  The beaus a balky team:
And when they wake, oh! how they'll shake
  To find it all a dream!
They'll think of wind, and fly, and flea;
But not of you! and not of me!
  Who cares? — I don't! — Do you?"

XXI.

Charm'd to hear, I bent me nearer; but, dismay!
    off dodged the toy,
Shaken, like a note of laughter, down the stiffening
    breath of joy.
"Cruel thing!" cried I, provoked then: "Witchery
    of condensed delight!·
Big Earth all too weak to find it, what an insult
    to the sight!"

XXII.

Soon I mused: this whole odd vision might be an
    imagined one:
Men had deem'd full half life's fabric, forms, by
    fever'd Fancy spun.
"Are all vain," at length I question'd; "do men
    dream thus. year on year,
See and hear, yet no real footsteps, naught to rouse
    the eye or ear?"
"Men who live by sight," she answer'd, "doubt it;
    but no doubt can sear
Back of proof a live conviction, that some Spirit-
    world is near:
And men feel it, all alone, and when the midnight
    hour is pass'd,
And they feel it when uprightness bends before too
    pressing blast:
Conscience! 'tis the soul's sensorium; God reveal'd
    to consciousness:
And remorse! the sinner cringing from the touch
    of Holiness.

XXIII.

"There is One, the heart knows truly, nor has heard of Him alone,
But of ranks, which grade all Being, upward toward the silent Throne,
Powers! — But they usurp no worship! Evil only would parade
Aught between the world's Creator and the smallest creature made.
And the evil? Ah! remember, when men overcome through prayer,
Not with flesh and blood they wrestle, but with powers which rule the air!
Helpt, far more than ofttimes conscious, by that Life which, all unseen,
Whirls the star, and waves the sea, and works the most self-govern'd mien;
And can send, for rare communion, clothed in raiment all too white
For the ken of mortal vision, those who force the fiend to flight."

XXIV.

We had left that field of fancy, and had reach'd a star-lit lawn,
And beyond its nether borders, Vapors, pallid from near dawn,
Cling about a crystal temple, rising from an ocean black,
Pure and restful pledge of promise, past the moody waves' attack.

Now we sail the mist-flung waters, cheer'd to watch where Clouds release,
Pedestal and pediment, and then entablature and frieze.
Darting 'neath high pearly pendants, and the great towers' jasper quoin,
We alight at lofty steps, and ranks of gold-mail'd wardens join;
Who, in stately silence parting, 'twixt the long lines pass us on
Toward the shimmering shields and sabres of a phantom garrison;
And the towering portico, a cliff of shafts, which far upheaves,
Till the very heavens seem suspended from its lordly eaves,
Drooping with thin starry mantle, deep below all mezzanine,
Whence aspiring Clouds, exhausted, seek, with zest, the fretful Brine.

XXV.

At its base a sire with thin locks gray through many a distant year,
Gazing 'neath the columns calmly, questions, as we venture near:
"Who is this you bring, my sister, who is this? Ah, yes! I trace
Restless eyes and flushing cheeks here; yes, ah yes, an earthly face!"
"One more youth, whose aspiration, as I rode full high at eve,

Craved for light; and, aided hither, would not now
    the portal leave."
"Aspiration," quoth he, mildly; "many a bitter,
    bitter Woe
Is begot by Aspiration. There are easier paths
    below.
He's the happy man who carries head not higher
    than his home,
'Tis right hard to stoop forever! But I keep you
    from the Dome."

XXVI.

At his bid, then, two, approaching, quick equipt me
    as a knight:
And they whisper'd, as they left me — "Faith alone
    can win the Light!"
When, at once, wide gates before us open'd, with
    a blaze of day,
And disclosed a hall resplendent, sweeping through
    long leagues away:
All about hung heavy incense, floating back to dim
    saloons,
Where half-hidden lamps swung star-like round the
    base of rare cassoons:
And dumb, caryatic figures, and chill columns, nude
    of wall,
Filed far off, like mighty sentries waiting for a
    funeral.
Through the clouds, which parted often, gleam'd,
    anon, mysterious bands:
And, from plinth to giant groin, resounded then,
    in low demands:

XXVII.

"Come to the Love, that is coming now,
  Come from the world away;
Come to the source of joy, and bow,
  Bow to the sweetest sway:
Love! for the wish that earth deceives;
Love! for the deed that goads and grieves;
Love! for the Heaven the soul receives;
  Love! and woe will away.

"Come to the Truth, that is coming now,
  Come from the world away;
Come to the source of right, and bow,
  Bow to the wisest sway:
Truth! for the thought that fails and fears;
Truth! for the deed that lives all years;
Truth! for the Heaven that ever cheers;
  Truth! and doubt will away.

"Come to Love and the Truth, attend,
  Come where Life's begun;
Whatever the source, whatever the end,
  Joy and the right are one.
Love! and the Truth shall brighter grow.
Truth! and Love shall warmer glow.
Love with Truth! and the soul shall know
  Christ! and the holy way.

"Come to Love and the Truth, attend,
  Come where Life's begun;
Whatever the source, whatever the end,
  Life and living are one!
Love! with a zeal that ne'er can rest,
Truth of the path that brings the best!
Love with Truth the home of the blest!
  God! and an endless day!"

XXVIII.

As the anthem ceast, — ah! music of such import
    has no death!
Evermore the tones refresh us, like a draft of angel
    breath! —
As it ceast, I sigh'd instinctive — "Would that I
    such bliss could share!"
When, behold, high, high uplifted, I was borne along
    the air,
On, and on, with slippery swiftness, sliding still to
    swifter flight;
Where the tall, white columns stalk past, like
    gigantic ghosts of night!
Where the arches fall and heave up, like the soul
    of some lost Sea!
Where the lamps streak by, a-quiver! — lines of
    morning on the lea!
Till came dawns of growing splendor! jambs, which
    burn'd all nearer air!
Quick degrees of soft arresting! and a broad ro-
    tunda there!

XXIX.

Broad it was, and high, and builded, lavish of the
    wealth of space, —
As all else had been, — a marvel, even in that won-
    drous place!
Such a sight Creation's Dawning saw, when, out
    infinity,
Morning mists exhaled to mingle with the azure,
    that should be:

Each diverse abaculus, as bright of gleam, as Chaos-mere!
Every torus pure and perfect, grand as embryonic sphere!
Then, with lines of earthly beauty, but recall'd to canonize,
Pillars, rivalling resurrection, soar'd to meet resentless skies.
Far above, the fickle flutings merged in spectral capitals:
And, within the shadowy volute, hover'd hosts of terminals;
Things of life or carved, I knew not, but, to my confused suspense,
They were holy from high distance: and I bow'd in reverence.

xxx.

Underneath the great dome's centre rose a form, most like a throne,
With bright outlines scarce distinguish'd, for a Cloud reign'd there alone.
And about its base an altar stretch'd, environing; a mound,
White; and reach'd by steps stupendous, grown like coral from the ground,
Toward the sides, where bulky panels sank to grasp, 'mid shifting smoke,
Figures!—whence?—what life, when carved, had loom'd to guide their sculptor's stroke?
Whose?—that course disclosed, as if quick sight itself did petrify

Forms of bliss, which bend and point for one who hardly yet can spy;
Lands which lure to peerless grandeur o'er an ocean rough and bare ;
Harbors near, whence crowds entice, past rocks and wrecks just hidden there ;
Ruder seas still wrestled bravely, worn to weary calm awhile ;
And a clear'd expanse of beauty greeting him who scans to smile ;
Then low storms on harsh horizon, brooding woe with darkening frown ;
And beyond, large heavenly mountains, where the tempests cringe adown ; —

XXXI.

Whose ? — But cloud fell covering these scenes : it was offspring of the fire
Living on the shrine, and lighting all the dome ; nor then to tire ;
Still unspent, I saw it press beyond through aisles, 'as bright as noon,
Startling thence, from far retirement, many a strange seductive boon,
Shapes on walls by Fresco fabled, myths reveal'd to reverent eyes ; —
What chill marble had congeal'd, clear rills of thought from Paradise.
Endless seem'd these aisles ! and countless ! built to meet, around the dome,
Radiated light, far-glancing, like the dawn from ocean foam !

XXXII.

Then came statement, that "The aisles, I watch'd with wish so masterless,
Held high limners' recollections of the hosts of holiness;
Who, on earth, pursued right purpose; follow'd, constant to the tomb;
Enter'd that; and thence, emerging, rested past all realms of doom.
Truth had no one mould for virtue; if I wish'd, I might select
Any course, and might explore it: and, when distant, could detect
What awaits the one who trusts such, when, of meaner means bereft,
Life is summon'd to move forward, with the Spirit only left."
So directed, I walk'd onward, reason lambent by the glare
Of designs, so dense and diverse, some I marvell'd should be there,
For they seem'd too fraught with pleasure; and I pass'd, without debate;
Sweet to 'mort exhaustion only are the drafts, which recreate.

XXXIII.

But, erelong, I came to opening, where a toilful wealth of walls
Told of memory of marts; and far-exalting council halls;

Where low throngs of coaches, winding 'neath wide elms toward mansions bold,
And bow'd, venerating faces symbolized the worth of gold.
"Truth," thought I, "needs place to prosper; and all earth obeys the voice,
That commands earth's richest treasure: I will make the gold my choice."
Quick as thinking this, I enter'd, and, a moment more, did stray
Through a scene of wild enchantment! it was Blessing's holiday!
But, beyond that, twilights gather'd; sallow waned the painted joys;
'Mid the shades gloom'd vice and sickness, coffins, ghosts, and gambling boys!
Rose a roar of floods before me! sight and sound for horror vied!
And I turn'd, a-shudder! nowhere, nowhere, now, was light to guide!
Far seduced thus from the altar, long I sought it, faint with fear,
Ere I spied, then, pondering, wonder'd how it was I lost me here?
What all meant — first woe? then darkness? and, so thinking, it did seem
Death was blackness and a night, where earthly glitter does not dream.

XXXIV.

Free from this, an aisle allured, so bright I could but make it mine!

There were books whence youth collected clean-cut precepts, line on line;
And, with pensive power embodied, life breathed in by Godlier men,
Matter, magnetized by touch of nervy chisel, brush and pen.
To my joy, the whitest statues lined the hall; o'er each was crown
Set with gems; and these held light which shined the whole far space adown.
"Here," cried I, "is what is wanted! Why was I so blind before?
Here's the distance all illumined!" and I hasten'd to explore.
Grandly, then, the glowing statues rose along the lengthening aisle;
And dreams, wing'd as by their spirits, bore me past my years the while,
Dreams of self, as ne'er forgotten, but in younger memory still
Throned a living Recollection, sceptred o'er some future Will!
Life! life! life! — deny it not, — we're made for Immortality!
Claims, which in the heart swell largest, look to longest destiny!
While I moved, unseen, the jewels stole and spent each other's light,
Introducing dusk to darkness, dodging doubt to crawling night.
Then cold mists arose embracing, and again the waters black

Hiss'd behind the tired amazement, slowly stumbling
toward the track.
"Ah!" sigh'd I, "those crowns! — that brilliance
burns but by a borrow'd might:
Stars themselves could guide us never were the
light less Infinite.
All that brightness lost in wandering! — there's but
one source, whence it came.
Arts ingenious catch and glance it, but the diamond's not the Flame!"

XXXV.

This time, when I reach'd the great dome, I remain'd somewhile doubt-bound,
Pledged to lengthy test, ere trusting any hall, whatever found;
But near by was place where many linger'd working, and I thought
That less lonely; and I spied, too, those, far off, with lights, who wrought.
So I paused and watch'd one, sketching what snug, slumbering Water dreams
Of the noiseless Clouds, attending slender wants of suckling Streams:
Flowers dependent, wait beside it: then mild vales of misty green
Reach to tops of Heaven-high mountains: — there are some white shrouds between: —
And, one side, where summer meadows melt to yield the golden grain,
From full school-house, lads and maidens throng to aid tired farmer swain:

Nigh to them are chariots waiting. and a sire from work doth rise,
Greeting Princes from far city, with diploma for the wise.
"General learning! honor'd labor! here," said I, "is equity:
Here truth ripens into duty — in the land, like nature, free!
And, as long as good lives, must live that which every joy foreran,
Love humane! too Godly high for slight of him whom God made man!"
Where so many work'd I enter'd: they did lessen one by one.
And upon the walls? — Zeal crowding, hinted hatred! strife begun!
Wrong that raged! and track'd a better! revolution, past reform!
Bringing sword! flame! smoke! destruction! and again light died in storm!
Deeply sad was my despair now: I could try no other aisle:
But I sat me down and wept, to think that Love, too, could beguile.

XXXVI.

Yet, at last, my heart, still anxious, moved me one more course to seek;
And I turn'd first toward the altar, there, when courage dared to speak,
Faintly questioning, "Oh, tell me, is there not some way all bright?"

"Yes," said One, " and they who find it, find what
    cannot end in blight."
Then, I thought, if in all reason be but one superior Choice,
Surely it could tarry never, summon'd by so kind a voice!
And, I cried, "Oh! Being Blessed, if an endless home this be,
Only breathe one word to aid me; I will ever serve but Thee!"

XXXVII.

He replied, then, "Are you kneeling? well for those who kneel in youth.
Self-reliance falls in failure, but the humbled rise with truth.
Yet dream not for gleams of wisdom, lightening everything before:
For advance of one still finite, there must still be waiting more.
Only signals can be given, these attended, by-and-by,
Through the pure, white air of heaven, shall emerge much mystery."

XXXVIII.

With these words an altar Server, at the glance of His desire,
Brought a ring, where, like a brilliant, burn'd light from the Holy Fire,
And upon my finger placed it, saying, "Everything's your own!"

Choose the way that seems the brightest! choose
    and act — as all — alone!"
Nearest was the aisle of riches; and, when far
    within, behold
That which shades had render'd woeful! 'twas the
    very Heaven of gold!
And the floods that I had fear'd so! — waters at the
    temple's side
Weirdly bright! with still more beauteous, near
    shores luring o'er their tide!
And the other aisles? — their story was the same!
    Ah me! 'tis strange
How the lights we carry with us make the scenes
    about us change!

XXXIX.

After Truth, thus far discover'd, as I sought the
    shrine once more,
Forms of glory gather'd round me, thousands there
    not seen before!
Bright they were to indistinctness! and bright rai-
    ment gave they me:
And within the folds were jewels it had dazzled
    Noon to see!
And my whole soul felt the nearness of that Love
    which lives with rest,
Free of faith, and full of welcome, from communion
    of the Blest.
Then, anon, I found me joining in desire, aroused
    awhile
By far stars, whence souls untiring seek the limits
    which exile.

Last, at sight of one just dawning, breathed a thought of harmony,
Sweet with all Love's Spirit-substance, melting forth to melody!

XL.

" See, along the azure creeping,
 See the World! its ransom reaping,
 Leaving sinning, glory winning,
  Through the ever brightening way.
 Oh for Bliss, the deeds of duty
 Rival boldest boast of beauty!
 Onward wend: with steadfast spinning,
  Learn to turn a perfect day.
  Work cannot be dark for aye.
  Woes but roll to roll away.

" World of Faith, the years are dying,
 Wherein clouds about thee lying
 Robe a wondrous waste of sighing,
  Empty throes of vain unrest.
 Be life right, whate'er now bearing,
 Right endures, when wrong is wearing:
 Right remains, when shrouds are tearing:
  Faith receives a full bequest;
  Wrestles through its prayer for rest;
  Dwells with Good, a constant guest!

" World of Hope, all power provoking,
 Reign of Light, all life invoking,
 Cheers thee on. Tho' gloom thy cloaking,
  Girt it is with rainbow belt.
 Days, when sun and soil are blending,
 Golden threads from heaven wending,
 Knit a wealth of thought extending
  Round about for promise dealt.
 Night! it blest the soul who felt,
 'Twas a star in which he knelt!

"World of Love, Heaven bends above thee:
Fear not clouds; it can but love thee.
Cherish'd child, if care is galling,
   Transient care is endless gain.
Oh there's growth of fadeless power,
Nursed by Vapors hour on hour!
Soon the time shall come, recalling
   No experience sent in vain.
   Fruit! 'tis that which fills the plain
When the stormy seasons wane!

"Onward World, move onward ever!
Love can be the loser never:
Truth and Error soon shall sever:
   Onward press thy mission through!
Holy Deeds thy dangers lighten!
Holy Words thy wisdom righten!
Holy Scenes, they come to brighten!
   Angel wings thy way pursue!
   Powers Divine direct anew!
   Peace is dawning down the blue!"

XLI.

Round and round me swell'd the chorus, like a spring to cleanse all space:
Widest waves, it seem'd to lift me, down! down! down! I fell apace.
Then, while suddenly the prospect broaden'd out, one blazing sea,
Startling into vague awaking, lo! those dear delusions flee!
Modest Sleep, that mused so sweetly, 'neath that star-gemm'd canopy,
Had been borne far down the west; and, pledged to ceaseless constancy,

Follow'd Day, in burnish'd armor, and with suite, all worn by fight,
Still to search, and search for ever for the shrinking forms of Night.
"Yes! 'tis dawn! it's killed my dreaming!" sigh'd I, as in dew and rill,
All the van of early Sunbeams shot reflections from the hill.
"But a dream!" I moan'd. Then, rousing, Thought essay'd, as if to find
Whither turn'd those phantom feet, that left such sunny track behind.

XLII.

And! — oh blest frank trust of boyhood! When the soul's young spring wells high;
When, within its depth is mirror'd life reflected from the sky;
Blest the faith in that life mirror'd, tho' from hight, one cannot scan;
Blest the faith, that, with corruption, man alloy'd, remains a man!
Yes! if always strive His Spirit, till all floods o'erwhelm the clod,
Infidelity to self is infidelity to God!
Perfidy to deeper nature, where, amid abounding ill,
Love, the magnet strong for loving, finds some truth incarnate still;
Truth, diffused through high and humble, finitely for finite par;
Yielding each a part alone, however bright, whoe'er they are!

XLIII.

And the whole? — it would grow plainer, could contentious Zeal advance,
Where impartial Wisdom questions e'en the portion of Romance.
It may be, more right is gather'd through the glance, too wild of scheme,
Than where stupid, prim Compliance nods and naps, without a dream.
It may be, more right's imparted through the love, too free of trust,
Than where mad Intolerance gags a pleading Doubt, with naught discust.
Men, who rouse to revolution, choosing stop and key to press,
Sweep their chords to swell a passion, pent in every consciousness.
Men, who range for reformation, fail of victory, till they see
Both the Truth array'd against them, and the Lie! for Charity,
First in logic, as in worship, leads the mind's triumphant train!
Follow Christ! ere Aristotle! sway the power below the brain!

XLIV.

Earth is man's; but Eden God's, which schemes that lost cannot restore:
Stretch'd for gods, men dwarf to devils! Time to trust to nature more!

Seek from friend and from opponent, truth obtain'd
    with candid eye,
Pure philosophy, supported by some part, which
    each supply,
Pillars this side, pillars that side, all for temple
    rear'd to God,
Let it rise, till light from Heaven cap acquirements
    of the sod !
There, the saint and sage together, at the shrine
    of faith shall bend ;
And the boons of better living round the dimless
    dome extend.

XLV.

Truth is broad but man is finite. Wide as wish,
    the worldly call ;
Wide as worlds, the cry for helpers, but one can-
    not turn to all.
Love, when souls are truthful only, trusts for ray
    of Higher Light,
Friend for worth, and foe for weakness, and its
    self, to prompt aright !
With the least light, what remaineth ? If a twinkle
    for an aim,
What but work despite disaster ? work, to save the
    wish from blame ?
Perfect methods, sure of wisdom, no experience
    can attain :
Faith, the source and sum of struggle, bringing
    failure, brings to gain :
He, alone, can hope to prosper, who, to reach per-
    ceptions rare,

Bravely girds, and ventures on, to be! to do! at least to dare!

XLVI.

What was my work? Toward the heaven morning clouds rose brightening there;
Toward the heaven, thought rose brightening, first to faith, and then to prayer!
Ere it ceast, the farm call sounded; and I sprung, as oft of yore;
But, along the well-plow'd hillocks, moved a Power, unfelt before;
And the wayward Whims of boyhood eagerly flock'd round to scan,
Where the Child, who dream'd at evening, went, at morn, to be the Man.

RE.

NEXT young among the voluntary scribes —
   Were one to judge by tones of voice alone —
Was a born prince of all authority.
Had he no right to it? Oft would friends say
That "if the boy could wait, gain gentleness,
He might grow a wise gentleman; besides,
Force, force was something, and he had force now;
So if" — of course no joke, but then it pleased —
That if — like Wisdom's best joke, all the town;
Threw up his mother's head, his sweetheart's down,
And tipt his rivals, like the winning yacht
Just rounding, with a last lurch, at the goal.
Still, stormy, thunder-lightning-zeal had he,
Bursting like bustling winds that blow in spring,
To fright, with death-white frost, life-color'd flowers,
And wreck each sail that dare presume for aid.
'Twas said one fairly gasp'd to hear him read —
His way to triumph! once sway'd by that speed,
Still faster endward each did wish he'd speed.
All gave the self-pleased boy what you have seen,
Taxt like their mirrors still and still to heed,
Nice men give — asking naught from — girls, young too.

POEM SECOND.

DARING.

I.

LO, long and lonely, stretch'd o'er hill and dale,
 Wrapt in her misty robe, reclines the Night;
No cloud, no leaf a-stir; moon small and pale;
 And stars scarce twinkling through the frosty light.
Earth sleeps; save that about the sea shore white
Weak Waves are whispering of some distant Gales;
 And timid insects, bold where none affright,
Whose hearts out-beat their fear, lisp loving tales,
Secrets they dare not breathe while Sunbeams scout the vales.

II.

But hark! 'mid stillness now a nervous tread
 Steals on the dews, a-shiver through the grass.
What form, pursued by what presaging dread,
 Speeds to escape this innocent morass?
 It is a youth whose eager mien, alas,
Bespeaks desire too deep for doubtful years.

Anon he pauses, and through tiny glass
Far backward scans ; then, tho' no life appears,
Anon, with haste renew'd, hies from renewing fears.

III.

He flies from home ; not first nor last, I ween,
    Forsaking friends for Midnight's chill embrace :
Not first nor last whom dawning day has seen
    A wanderer, stay'd by no familiar face.
    Say Homes bereaved ! can long years e'er displace
The melancholy vacancy of hours
    When memory strays aback, with painful pace,
Whither life bloom'd to promise such sweet flowers,
Ere one harsh storm snapt off the buds that blest your bowers ?

IV.

Ah sad to find the germ of love and care
    Grow but to sting the hand that would caress !
Still sadder the lone dearth of that despair
    No more retaining life it would redress !
    Yet, here, one hope remains, — that, when some stress
Of needful years provoke to earnest plan,
    A headstrong will, in youth so masterless,
May rouse, with sovereign power to sway his clan,
From mood with spirit high, inspiring strength for man.

V.

Think not a paltry purpose stirr'd the soul
  Of him now hastening o'er this dusky plain.
His was a youth whence fancy spied a goal
  For good alone, that gleam'd and gleam'd amain
  Where fact each morn beheld each effort vain.
For this, all else his spirit had resign'd,
  Deep-sworn the one bright object to attain,
Through deeds of present life to bless mankind,
And for the future leave a standard pure behind.

VI.

His was a state where freedom's dawn did bring
  With widening views of beauty, those of blight.
There manhood reign'd ; and each, enthroned a king,
  Made wrong more wrong through more of oversight ;
  A nation his, where race a race could slight,
With ill in self, and in the things it brought ;
  For man is man, whatever hue or hight ;
And long as laws allow free, truthful thought,
'Tis but through general good, a nation's can be wrought.

VII.

In such a land, Emancipation's need
  Had made unconscious of one other due
Full many a wiser soul that moved to deed.
  The Slavery there — the ward of patriots too —
  They felt a foe, that bode his time, and grew :
They sought not Statesmanship, with mouth to frame

VIII.

The youth, scarce heeding where he was or went,
   Moved wildly on as thoughts that work'd his will;
As if, tho' meager means might soon be spent,
   Proud Hope could feel unborn successes thrill;
   Till resting on the brow of higher hill,
His face betokens that vain fears dispel;
   And, gazing back, he stands a moment still;
But soon emotions, from full fountains swell;
And utter thence a fond and passionate farewell:

IX.

"Ye mountains, vales, and bays, and woods, and streams, —
   Oh never, never seem'd ye half so rare!
How beauteous each shall wake when morning gleams!
   Yet I who love you so shall not be there!
   But ne'er shall I forget the guise ye wear,
So long as thought shall roam, or love be free. —
   Why are not souls proportionately fair?
Ah, then, how fill'd with joy might all things be?
And then there were no need that ye should banish me!

X.

"And yon hot hut, beside those stunted oaks,
   Long smothering all the dear desires of youth,

Dream not I shall regret your yards and yokes
   Who go to harvest broader fields of truth !
A fiercer curse than ever comes, forsooth,
When morning light reveals my vacant cell —
   Will one be sad ? — Ah William, is it ruth
To leave you thus ? forgive me, 't is the spell
Of strange sensations here ! yes, yes I must, fare-
      well ! "

XI.

Ask you, why I who write look up and seek
   The face which from the mirror glances down ? —
This is not he who, fed by fancies' freak,
   Grew out the limits of his native town.
   About those lips and eyes a fickle clown
Of hope was sporting : here, tired memories rest.
   That form bent not before stern Fortune's frown :
Nor round that head had throng'd each ghostly
      guest —
God grant white harbingers of crown not manifest !

XII.

A few short years, how will their sun and storm
   Trail marks of change across the face and frame ;
And what one vaguely deems himself, transform
   To second self, both friend and foe disclaim !
   And, in the heart, how unmark'd calls for fame,
Where once the young blood sprung at each fresh
      drum !
   Those shifting thrills of hope and fear, how
      tame ! —
Familiar throbs of life's old pendulum,
Wound up to vibrate on till hope and fear be dumb.

XIII.

A few short years, ah, steady, steady grown,
    The fickle brook has reach'd the level mead
Where now, no more to boist'rous torrents thrown,
    The deeper current moves, with noiseless speed.
    And haply thus, altho' one may not heed
Full springs that start through tides far underneath,
    Yet wide to further still maturer deed,
More strong, tho' naught disturb its bordering heath,
Life works on worthily the surface calm beneath.

XIV.

The boy — for man to term the boy's life "I"
    Appear'd now false, and even half profane:
For sacred is that past he walks, where lie
    Lands bright with joy, and where all distant pain
    Flits, slight as shade, or beautifies, if lain——
The boy pass'd on; and just as dawn began
    To sketch far east a rare autumnal plain,
Along the road in front his eyes could scan
A house, and barn, and fence, on which there lean'd a man,

XV.

A farmer, o'er whose broad and sun-served brows
    Brown Health had laid her consecrating hands;
With stalworth shoulders bent by Toil that bows
    As mindful aye of boons from generous lands;
    With soul, ne'er swerved by scheme the loon commands,
Smiling from all the face a welcome true,

Through eyes attention wistfully expands,
Unwont to choose from books a mystic clew
And search the maze of self for phantoms ever new.

XVI.

He saw the youth; and, while a whistled song
  Flew off from opening lips, he thus began:
" Bright morning neighbor, judge it's pretty long,
  Your walk: you're plodding like a puritan.
  There must be something stirring in the van
That it can further such unusual zest?
  Where do you go? — Don't know? — Without a plan
As well await the sunset in the west? —
Well, well I never question; but you'll stop? and rest? —

XVII.

" Good farm you say? quite wise to think it is!
  No better land in all this hemisphere.
Grain grows so fast, one well-nigh hears it whiz!
  I've somewhat changed about the crops this year,
  But on my side-hill lot, just over here,
Where now these buckwheat buds puff out like leaven,
  Last fall the corn — I swear I speak sincere —
Stood fifteen feet, as tho' the Dung had striven,
Pelagian-like, to build green Babels up to Heaven!

XVIII.

" Some breakfast? Yes, of course. — But spare your cents,

  I have n't much ; to that I welcome you, —
Just ready. Early breakfasts save expense : —
  One's sooner through for work ; and eats less too."
  While seated at the board, with quick review
Of those brave resolutions he had made,
  The boy, to cause of reformation true,
Vow'd to commence at once to wield his blade :
But thus his host repell'd each venture he essay'd : —

XIX.

" Free slaves ? lift masses ? — nonsense ! — For the
   schools
  I'd pay my taxes, yes ; but not sure still
That men train working, and not talking, tools,
  Who ease of muscle and strain up of will.
  Better strong meat, like this. Pass up ; I'll fill
Your plate again. — Then take more hash ? — I'd
   vow,
  My boy, they'd wean'd you on a sugar-pill !
This creature was the most fat, soft, sweet sow
Whose furs e'er snugg'd the baby-worms. There,
   try that now.

XX.

" All men should learn ? — not as you state it, boy ;
  All men should learn enough to make them work.
A little less may now and then annoy ;
  A little more makes lazy as a Turk. —
  No, I do not like radicals ! No jerk
Can out-root all of evil in a trice :
  Wherever grain can ripen, weeds must lurk ;
And some grow till the harvest. Take advice :
Impatience cannot force these fruits of Paradise. —

XXI.

"Not philanthropic? — pugh! I tell the world: —
  'If they'll leave me alone, then I'll leave them.'
Last year, some city swells came out, and whirl'd
  Our country up-side down, with stratagem
    To rip a rattling railway through the hem
Of my farm here; tried to inflate the thing
  With long blown lies of cash. I said to them
'Do you pretend your nuisance wouldn't bring
All else your big town hatches with its dingy wing?

XXII.

"'Disinterested friends; this is a place
  For country rest: nor now, nor in next year,
Do we intend its quiet to efface
  By buzz and bustle of your boasted sphere.
    Besides — altho', perchance, a trifle queer —
We scarce propose to triple our expense
  Even for double gains of which we hear. —
When our good wives turn'd chrysalids of sense.
To burst, town butterflies! we'd rue the consequence!

XXIII.

"'And as for letters, news and active life,
  We've work'd these heaving hills enough, to know
On farm one finds sufficient storm and strife,
  And life full fast, tho' you imagine, slow.
    Content to watch the seasons come and go,
With each new sport and task by each one given;

With hunt for summer, and with sleigh for snow,
Match'd against smoky streets, all stench and
    steven,
We know, if out the world, we live much nearer
    Heaven!'

XXIV.

"Here! help me finish this raspberry pie;
  Right full of seeds!—but seeds, where sown,
    may grow?—
To church?—Yes always, when the clouds are
    high:
  I think as much of home and Bible tho.'—
  Not public-spirited?—Well, may be, no.
But mark me, boy, one way to influence
  Is to improve one's own! My thrift to show,
I don't blackguard my neighbor's, o'er the fence,
But make my place attract; and shame his differ-
    ence!

XXV.

"But half the truth?—What, going?—Better rest?
  Brows always knit grow wrinkled in their prime.
Must?—Then good-bye; perhaps it may be best:
  But pardon one more word,—tho', at your time,
  I too had whims that I too thought sublime,—
Don't be so bent to drive the older folk.
  If youth must hurry toward its wiser clime,
Let it goad on the young. It cann't provoke
Old heads, too long ago grown steady to their yoke!

XXVI.

"Farewell:"— Then hastening out, and through the
 path,
The guest soon disappear'd far down the way,
Where stormy feelings, more in woe than wrath,
 Dash'd to wet eyes, weak tributes of dismay:—
 "Alas, poor Tongue! and shall you ne'er convey
Conviction for the deeds you would install?
Where'er I'd rouse a soul that good have sway,
Whose fault, when lo! in answer to each call,
Jeers stalk, whence I had hoped that Love would
 marshal all!

XXVII.

"So was it on the farm: so is it here.
 But, on the farm, those brutal ways withstood
Because too unkind, kind deeds to revere.
 But this man seem'd so kind!"— thus did he
 brood,
 And who would not?— Where good men slight
 our good
There comes the worst test Faith can e'er out-pace.
 Well for the boy, doubt donn'd a mootish mood:—
If one who loved but self and not the race,
With so small thing to love, could wear so pleased
 a face?

XXVIII.

And where was youth, in whose uncertain breast,
 When good and ill were wildly balancing,

Brave hope for best did not outweigh the rest?
   And thus ere long, from grief recovering,
   He grew quite sure that years more skill would bring:
And that with other men, he would agree:
   This isolated farmer — no strange thing —
Had schemes for good, no doubt, the same as he,
But did not understand him; no, it could not be.

XXIX.

So he trod lightly on: and, when, at noon,
   The shades were folding in each sheltering wing,
He found beneath broad oaks a grateful boon,
   Five women dining round a sparkling spring.
   They offer food; then, after pain'd throats swing
In stiff suspense their tongues to bid him cheer,
   Thrill back to nature's gossip-caroling —
Their Joseph, fy! how qualm'd, how scared to hear
What horrid, scandalous pit he'd dared to venture near!

XXX.

Escaped this peril soon, he reach'd a town,
   One whence a railway stretch'd far toward the sea.
He enter'd a long train, and sat him down,
   First nervous, then right wild with ecstasy!
   The clatter timed old tunes! The trees, whirl'd by
And wheel'd far off, danced to the music's might!
   As towns and crowds sped past so rapidly,

Charm'd half to sleep, he dream'd all work'd for
   right :
And that all earth had grown so beautiful! so
   bright!

XXXI.

He was awaken'd out of reverie
   By two loud voices from the seat behind.
He turn'd and faced a man, whose glancing eye
   Now beam'd, as tho' with love for all mankind;
Then changed its look, as wandering to find
Regard for self, or thought to be repeal'd;—
   With knowledge of the world and doubt combined
Which gives to manners art, not all conceal'd;
To words, sound school'd to stay what should not
   be reveal'd.

XXXII.

Beside him sat another, all his face
   Sway'd by a courage bold to conquer care.
His glasses, shifted oft with easy grace,
   Great coat, large pockets, and abundant hair
   Mark'd him — "physician," one whose sovereign air
Rebukes the rage of fevers into rest,
   Whose brow can bear unmoved the anxious stare,
While children wilder o'er his crowded chest;
And how a silent pulse can tell which cure is
   best?

XXXIII.

The first one, from his conversation, seem'd
   Thought from commercial spheres to intimate:—

"I much regret our old friend should have deem'd
  His special calling now, to advocate
  These strange reform bills; if he could but wait,
His talents might prove par for any place
  In all the land. Discounting at this rate,
Trust me, they'll reach, ere long, a day of grace
With every note of fame protested by the race."

XXXIV.

The other said: — to skip words harsh for rhyme —
  "All very true: a ventricle should not
Out-act an auricle: there was a time,
  Place, ad captandum vulgus: this was what,
  In actu, made men: he never forgot
His diagnosis, Medicinæ D.,
  Not D. D.: some, for instance, told a sot,
Most dead, the truth; to wholly kill: not he;
Nor thought a devil's tool could — delve respectably."

XXXV.

He paused to gaze upon the open eyes
  And mouth of the awed boy who sat before;
Increasing much the listener's surprise
  By questioning: what thoughts he held in store? —
  Who blush'd and turn'd, but summon'd, o'er and o'er,
Answer'd, at first, with timid, modest tone:
  "Perhaps he did not understand their lore;
But, if he did, at least he dared to own
But little could it please them if those thoughts
  were known."

XXXVI.

'Gainst this, they both made protests, moved by which
   The boy much love for truth and freedom spoke.
As ways waxt bold, the doctor seem'd to hitch
   His questioning thought with words, no sense could yoke,
Altho' his comrade found full many a joke.
Anon appear'd the purpose of the twain,
   In interchange of glance. Then patience broke.
'Tis test of brightest zeal, if quib profane,
Back, like a mirror's flash, the insult flies again.

XXXVII.

"Had I not seen enough," he said, "to show
   Your vile hypocrisy without this test?
Must you add dung to dirt, and foully grow
   Rank insult from filth, else too manifest?
   Yes, yes I was a fool, I own, to rest
A confidence in men, too mean to know
   With what sublimer views those souls are blest
Who look away from self! If self below
Seem bright! so does the devil! brilliant as his woe!"

XXXVIII.

His quivering mouth could hold no further word:
   Nor was there need: the two soon left the train.
"A strange and saucy stripling!" this he heard,
   Then he was left alone, alone with pain.
   They did not know how oft and oft amain
Hot tears came seething from his boiling breast;

Nor think how wit, wing'd warbling from one brain,
May build on tender souls a loathsome nest,
Pluck slowly dying leaves, and brood, o'er long unrest.

XXXIX.

Then too the young are true philosophers,
  For aye retaining all impartially
To graft in thought and grow in characters.
  When learning sates a spare necessity,
  A man may deem his small advance a plea
For crampt contentment with too little lore,
  Or fatted pride, wind-blown ere victory:
But very few are children ever more,
To trace with simple faith the wonders still before.

XL.

And he thus left — no words, however sad,
  Could speak his grief, nor any fancy show.
What fathoms that wild source that can make mad?
  What is it swamps the reason, when below
  Dark depths of fancy well to overflow?
What latent power of grief impels them on?
  When, 'midst fierce storm-clouds, ghosts of buried woe
And future ill conjure, with features wan,
Sensations too acute for thought to poise upon?

XLI.

"I wonder if it be that yon pale star
  Shines now on those I love?" so mused he here: —

"Those dear old faces!—strange how dim they are!
   And can it be they nevermore shall cheer?—
   A fool was I, to let, without a tear,
Such fruitless hope outweigh a bliss possess'd!—
   And are they joyous there, tho' I'm not near?
Or do they weep with kindred woes oppress'd?
Or is naught kindred now for this lone, shivering breast?

XLII.

"On either side, I hear, 'mid nod and smile,
   From festive hearts, this ringing laughter bound—
I'd rather be the wretch who, down the aisle,
   From coffin seal'd, cries—'murder!' to the sound
Of his own requiem! 'twere sweet compound
To mine!—who'd mourn for me? for me, a pest?
   Why all things shun me:—e'en this senseless ground.—
How far away the chill night sears the west!
How very, very far mild Nature's mocking rest!

XLIII.

"A tale, I've read, of one spared spar that bore
   A shipwreck'd sailor far from friendly lea,
Nor heeded beacon-fires upon the shore
   That flared and fell while swell'd and sank the sea.
Ah! there be things leave Earth more direfully:—
These woes that float back deathward through the brain
   Where storms that will not let the dying be

Surge up as tho' with new impulse of pain,
   To crack each shatter'd nerve, and burst each
      straining vein.

XLIV.

"Yet far, cold world, I love! could I not show
   Some soul, that out its usual quest would veer,
That they yield most to friends whose love can flow
   But for the few? — Alas! shall such appear?
   Is desolation dear to lure them near?
Is woe so worthful, it can woo Delight? —
   Oh God! spare one, one chording voice! — I hear
Heaven's full of chords to diapason might
Of love, with common base deep in the Infinite!"

XLV.

The train had stopt: and out the crowd there came
   A youth who after many a bow and smile,
And parting and return, to make the same,
   With curious eye came sauntering down the aisle,
   Then sat beside our wanderer. "Not much style
Aboard!" said he. "Confound my ears! — A bore,
   A blasted bore, this tunnel! I could file
Two beauties past blear-eyed coquets, three score,
Without such clatter! — Why, what's up? You're
      looking sore?

XLVI.

"A little blue? — that's up enough! sky-high!
   Felt so myself! Seen stars sometimes! Why hide
The cause? Take the hide off. By my best eye

To flay a folly slays it. A rawhide
  Peels a fool's thought, moults foolish! Come,
    confide?
Naught like an airing, would you oust a moan."
  Our youth look'd longing toward his proffer'd
    guide,
For those strange words had yet a friendly tone;
And, as he watch'd that face, he seem'd no more
    alone:

XLVII.

Besides, he had no great trusts to confide,
  So soon imparted them to this new friend,
On whom not some but all appear'd to glide:
  Would God our older cares found such an end!
  "That all your cash? and bound to try a bend
To New York? Quite a crazy crook! for what?
  To make a man? A project to commend
At your size! Not a fascinating sot
That held you bound! But let unfruitful topics
    rot:

XLVIII.

"I have a guardian — honor to whom due!
  He guards what shops are paid, I, what they
    sell.
This governor rules a school: that should suit you,—
  And a gazette, that shouldn't! — funereal! —
  Taste, Truth, both sacrificed to th' riff-raffs' hell!
Could you spell out goose-tracks of genus coy;
  Stop up each sense; without cold, snivel well,

So that to him like tone like slang convoy,
He's seen so much of me, he'd have another boy."

XLIX.

Then added he of life in Baltimore,
  "In that right merry State of Maryland : —
No Yankee-made strait-jackets to restore
  The souls gone mad from endless reprimand ! —
  All the best fun on earth their town could stand,
Tho' 'ad made — for hens, with half-hatch'd hopes waylay'd —
Black abolition speeches contraband —
Don't frown, a slave's not such an ugly jade.
And boy, my boy, you'll find there many a bright eyed maid."

L.

The boy had frown'd ; but 't was the frown of dreams,
  When blinded sight shies from too dazzling light.
For here up-gleam'd the acme of his schemes : —
  To know the South, and learning, learn, to write.
  It distanced hope he had not dared excite.
He e'en forgets his mission while he bends
  To catch the wild details, so swift of flight,
About that new-found home, and coming friends,
While Fancy each strange form, a stranger halo lends.

LI.

He hears about the school ; "the queerest set
  Earth e'er had jarr'd together ; down from Pool —
The pest of tutors, but the student's pet,

Who works all day but never with the school,
  Gains discipline through zest and not through
    rule —
Way down to Sims, whose ample pocket-toys
  Outweigh the brain, a fop and fawning fool,
Dons vice by nature, doffs but when decoys,
The beau of all the girls, the butt of all the boys."

LII.

Then of a matron : — " snarling, sharp, and slim :
  A thing best made to punch with ! topt by hue
Of blood too ! with a gait as stiff and prim
  As stilts could give ! who eats with chronic —
    ' pshew ! '
  Lest bad breath taint her — mirror ! for the
    shrew
Has no friends : like a caged beast's sentinel,
  Pokes up all day a snarling brat or two ;
Or hints a deal of news she must not tell ;
Or finds out all folk do, and not one doing well."

LIII.

Then of a tutor : and that tutor's life,
  'Spite all the funny traits young wit could show,
Loom'd like a chieftain's form to fainting strife —
  This seem'd the soul the boy had yearn'd for
    so : —
" A man who loved a ' yes,' but dared say ' no ! '
Strict, yet with smiles ; gay, yet a Christian too.
  'Twas said he'd weather'd many a storm below,
Still vigor stay'd ; and, when in spirits — whew !
You'd think he'd gulpt down each, to blow its sport
    for you ! "

LIV.

Some men there are, whose generous zeal for truth
   Burns like that holy bush which Moses saw,
To leave each leaf and limb still green with youth :
   Some souls there are, impell'd by love, not law.
   Dear thence the boon from living wells to draw
The deep experience stored through strife unseen.
   Sweet are the words, pure past all fear of flaw,
From melting hearts, with naught to intervene
'Twixt mind and mouth to mould them cold, tho' crystalline !

LV.

Such was the soul, our youth, soon after, found
   Prepared to aid the groundwork of his thought :
And oft, when delving down where doubts abound,
   The wisest way, by that wise friend was taught.
   He loved his work, aye feeling, while he wrought,
That only from the deep foundations rise
   Grand structures, like the model that he sought :
And tho' this oft was hid to drooping eyes,
Anon he'd spring to see it flash from clearest skies !

LVI.

Then would he live for months in that bright land
   Where boyhood dwells, to bless perpetual morn ;
Where 'mid the fragrant air on either hand
   Throng birds and buds and sunbeams newly born ;
   Where care whiffs by like wind ; and every thorn
That paves the path o'er which the feet must stray
   Gleams 'neath the dewy crystals that adorn,

With thousand charms to dazzle down the way,
And rouse far drawn desires this earth can ne'er allay.

LVII.

He lived, with deepening eye, and merry voice,
   And winning ways that grew still more in grace,
To laugh from chance but be demure from choice,
   While 'mid each form he sought to find some face,
   And through each sound some subtle thought to trace :
For this, he oft would search, 'mid dust and noise,
   Strange buildings or the queerer populace ;
And wend where on the green the crowd enjoys,
And mourns and mocks by turns, young soldiers and old boys.

LVIII.

Or, sicken'd by the crime and filth one meets,
   He'd wander nervously adown the hill,
Along the shady side of grand old streets,
   To reach the sea, and gaze in waters still,
   Or skip smooth pebbles through each rising rill,
Long charm'd, he knows not wherefore, by the play ;
   Then seek his bed to rise, when white stars thrill
With feelings wide and wild which melt away
With bells whose echoes bound like breakers 'round the bay !

LIX.

At times, grown sad for lost hours, nights would find

Him dashing through the course of some chance book
The fickle passion of unbridled mind.
Alas! how many truths did he o'erlook!
How many rich-robed lies for guides he took!
How dizzy love grew, lured by glittering wing
Through morbid fantasy! How sweet Faith shook,
Half kill'd by darts, well nigh too sharp to sting,
Thrust through the back by those who spoke so mild a thing!

LX.

But books brought good with bad. From doubting task
That incantation came for each truth sought,
Which may fail all, but least fails those that ask,
So long as conscience grow with growing thought.
Howbeit, when Pride would taunt crude ways untaught,
Or Prejudice laugh down some odder scheme,
He fear'd for self that argued now, now fought;
But soon forgot the thing, for higher theme,
In doubt then if the woe had been in deed or dream.

LXI.

More oft, impell'd by wild unrest within,
Half wrong, half right, he sought to sate its might
Through trumpet-blasts of onset to all sin:
Or real, or fancied, both invoked his spite.

He storm'd the seen! he stabb'd that out of sight!
A young Don Quixote, caring first to dare,
  He harm'd more good, perchance, through zeal for right,
Than lie or sham, his effort could lay bare:
He stirr'd the most of dust just where most need of air.

LXII.

And this he found; for one sweet day when all
  His soul had seem'd to bloom in dreams most bright,
He waked, to note near shadows crawl the wall,
  And, turning quickly, met the welcome sight
  Of fondest friends, long wont to cheer when Right
Urged knightly wish to tilt some erring soul.
  'Spite strife to check them, lo! 'mid laughter light,
His own name toss'd! Oh God! with grace control
Faith, finding first how near Life skirts a trustless shoal!

LXIII.

What lover dreams that love which throbs and thrills
  Can, for one heedless hour, be laid aside?
The heart of that soul-life, whose beating fills
  Each individual ripple of the tide
  Of blood or breath, where has the soul-life died?
Ah, when, swift stirr'd, it doffs this fleshy vest,
  Love, like the lightning, flash'd from storms, shall glide

To join full light of heaven! tho' all the rest
Fall back, as clouds, that wept, sink, spent, on
    Ocean's breast.

LXIV.

"My Pythias?" he heard:— "He's like a Muse,
    The more unseen the more inspiring, oh!
I deem some friends like onions;— best to use
    When one's alone;— or else with geese;— not
    so?
Come, here's a problem:— you are stumpt to show
Just where the fellow's like a goose?"— "Because
    He's good to pluck, with feathers white too!"
        "No."
"Well then, with chief defence — you see — his
    jaws, —
Good weapons only for a bird of cloven claws."

LXV.

"He cackles ere he scratches;— but go to!
    I judge that one a goose, whenever wont
To mix with men, who'll quack and hiss — you
    know —
    A-face the kitchen door, and not the front!
    Like one of Scott's grand soldiers in the brunt,
Who always saw the stranger wrong side first —
    With bad impression! Pshaw! to be so blunt
For good, so sharp for sin is to be curst.
They're bound to find but woe who feel but for the
    worst.

LXVI.

" 'Tis pity too. If he had aught below,
  Some wheeling years that pass might whet his
    wit:
But he's top-heavy. Whims upset him so;
  He's like a spinning top; — well whipt for it,
  He'll whine with wind; not whipt, have a moping
    fit!" —
This was too much: the boy could bide the rest.
  But when pretended friends could thus submit
His young life's failure for his whole life's test,
It was to doom for woe all hope that still seem'd
    blest.

LXVII.

He spoke: "It might be well for one who skims
  Only of surface thinking, not to mock
What lies too deep for him. I seem all whims.
  Tell how a body differs from a block,
  Except through these same whims? Be you the
    rock,
That staid, world-worthy thing, doomsday shall find
  Mud-bound! — I'd rather be the weather-cock,
To whine? — Yes whine! — clean-splinter with the
    wind!
If so some sign from heaven were token'd to my
    kind! —

LXVIII.

"Too late recalling words now! You were right —
  'Twas kind to be just, e'en behind one's back! —

The goose did hiss! Is't strange thing in your
    sight,
    Life, true to nature?—it hiss'd back a quack!
    Oh, I have seen lips, livid from long lack
Of what the heart held; truth and tongue had cut
    Connection; only aping left, my pack —
The witty apes were first of brutes, but tut!
They thought to mock true men, and turn'd creation's
    butt! —

LXIX.

"Spare me! for flattery, that whited scum
    Of selfish souls, taste sickens in the end.
'Tis not forever sweet, the modicum!
    Try a fresh tongue! To serve it, you can wend,
    Not hoof'd nor horn'd; some smooth mask, I'd
        commend;
Yet ne'er let slip the cheat; lest dupes begin
    To scorn! God-knighted Conscience will not bend
When one would praise himself; but stabs within.
And what self yields not self, it yields to no one's
    — sin!"

LXX.

Much more he might have rail'd; but, glancing
    up,
    Beheld his favorite teacher hear him chide!
Then soon the froth that foam'd above the cup,
    Dissolv'd in timid tears, stole down the side: —
    "Ah Sir, I could not help it. I could bide
A boast of Insult, if victorious Mirth
    Snatch'd not a victim's crown. Not only pride,

The good, one might do, bids defend self-worth.
That lost, and all is lost, all influence but dearth." —

LXXI.

I've read that, in old times, men sought the list,
  Of whom one mark'd the groundlings nudge and
    prate,
Because of humble guise — "Io Egotist!"
  There's many a modest soul must bear that fate
  Whom unobtruding worth has doom'd to state
Of low regard, which one faint sigh repels:
  Earth likes the swaggering, plumed, and spurr'd
    ingrate
Well cheer'd alone ere trump to onset swells;
But not one half-way protest! — get you cap and
  bells! —

LXXII.

Self may live far from its ideal ends,
  As earth from heaven; as dreams from love
    awake:
Then judge we self by wish; but nearest friends
  Judge but by works, and, judging thus, mistake.
  This boy deem'd his friend harsh, who strove to
    make
Now pride, now anger proof of love amiss:
  Then, when the injured heart still more would
    ache,
Gave it a book: — "A few hours spent with this
May train calm thought," he said; "and teach
  analysis."

LXXIII.

And such, when well prepared, thus read the youth:
  "The kindliest aim might fail, pumpt up like spleen
With gusty face and fist, e'en tho', forsooth,
  'Peace, peace on earth, good will toward men' the theme.
  Would one deal TRUTH for thought?—or LOVE for mien?—
TRUTH is best dealt through proof, as thus:—twice three
  Are six; we each have three, then six between:
A powerless form, knew not both equally
Twice three are six; did not proof start where both agree.

LXXIV.

"And thus it is that widest powers belong
  To liberal minds. They yield much to the race,
And gain much oneness thence to woo the throng.
  Real eccentricity moves off through space,
  Concentric ne'er! Shut in to self, a grace,
As brains entomb'd breed worms, breeds bigotry;
  Whence love's live spirit flies toward Heaven apace,
Where stars, tho' single, blend, a galaxy;
And wills blend, one through right divine of Charity.

LXXV.

"Treat not as fabrics of vain human wit
  The deepest moral truths. Believe the mind

Is dower'd with such when form'd. To benefit,
   Rouse first each germ already in mankind,
   For good grown outward from true life behind.
God's Spirit moves to love but one deep key
   Whence all life-music sounds. So power to find
'Mid minds or natures deepest harmony —
Genius grows chiefly such through geniality.

LXXVI.

" And if not TRUTH, but LOVE one deal; how then,
   Imparting spirit such as now redeems
Through kindlier weal the worth of modern men,
   Can strife attain one aim of loving themes?
   Can bitter sources flow to flood sweet streams?
If, stirr'd to grand endeavor, one would blend
   An anarchy of individual schemes
In Heaven-like union for harmonious end;
If union come through love, let love its claims
   commend.

LXXVII.

" Pause, where Reform would form to one fond truth
   All else, lest it court self, ideal-bright.
A new aim push'd despite old good forsooth,
   A finite aim adjusts not all things right.
   The gain complete is always Infinite!
The choice to serve but self made Adam fall,
   E'en wishing wisdom; and to mould through might
Others to self, cloaks with a tyrant's pall
The freedman's leader; and makes demons of us
   all.

LXXVIII.

" Remember One divine, and yet a guide,
　　Whose precious promises seem less command,
Than pæans which proclaim that strife subside.
　　Remember Moses when beneath the hand
　　Of God within the rock. What seem'd too grand
When with that Spirit's strength investitured ? —
　　Like them, to-day, all through the world might stand
Meek men, for whom had patient faith secured
More power than princes wield, of countless hosts assured.

LXXIX.

" Seek faith, for through the clouds that cover all
　　This looms the only archway toward the Throne.
The skill that sows the seed can never call
　　The grain to life; where'er the germ be grown,
　　'Tis vivified by power, to man unknown.
So till the earth; and learn, as storms revive,
　　Failure in toil were this, to toil alone.
Then strange 't will seem that men should wrongly strive
When love, that prompts mild aims, alone can make aims thrive."

LXXX.

" Well done ! " the master said : " Wise then, would all
　　Whom passion plunges into sudden ill,
Quick to resent, be as quick to recall.

Ere hating hours hatch habits, swift fulfill —
So Love may still seem sovereign of the will —
All friendliness to friends, Love yet may save.
And one thing more: before, o'er Eastern hill,
Comes broader light, think not Heaven to out-
brave :
Nor quite so wisely speak full freedom for the
slave."

LXXXI.

Some more he spoke ; then left with mild adieu. —
No human voice could now recall the dart
Love's Thoughtlessness, but of an instant, threw :
"False friends," the poor boy mused, "had heard
his heart!
His words were blamed, forsooth, for lack of
art!
What then? he could not, would not don disguise.
Blame were more blest than praise, from truth
apart!"
He sought his bed ; he dream'd, 'mid waking cries,
Of contest flaming up to smoke that hid the skies ! —

LXXXII.

Oh world, world, world! you play'd too well your
part,
When our ideal life first bade farewell
To Hope, low-framing towers of perfect art!
When from the scaffolding, Faith, fainting, fell
'Mid rocks so chill, and yet so near to Hell !
Poor Babel-dreams, what were our brains about?
No fancied forms to full proportions swell !

Comes reel! comes rack! then grim and ghastly
  doubt!
Why brood, black buzzard? why not rip the doom'd
  heart out? —

LXXXIII.

He seem'd to gaze aback the long, long years,
  Where chariot wheels that roll'd through ages
    past
Creak'd as with groans which shook far yawning
  fears!
  And all about were wars! no peace to last!
  Or tombs, with gilded praise to guilt most vast!
He sought the future; but from unform'd life
  Congealing chaos chill'd the brooding blast!
He fear'd to know what wrong, what right was rife!
He dared not look beyond thick fumes of earthly
  strife!

LXXXIV.

He woke: and mused of self. The wisest souls
  Muse first of self; mild, tho', so long denied,
They see, still far beyond, their chosen goals.
  But he, he was not wise yet, to confide
  In distant good. He thought how he had tried:
And self lost love: and others gain'd but pain:
  How he had spurn'd, — for wrongs he could not
    bide, —
His benefactors. What course could remain? —
One: — he must leave their roof tho' all his hopes
  be slain!

LXXXV.

He seized his clothes: and rush'd out through the
    night
  Where Darkness trembled 'neath the threatening
    tread
Of an advancing Storm. Oh fearful sight —
  That black car of the Thunderer overhead!
  Those fierce bolts flashing down their line of red!
And crashing on amid the scatter'd sleet!
  Whence one broad elm, like Cæsar stabb'd and
    dead,
Flung up its robes, and tumbled at his feet,
While hoarse winds howl'd about, a fiendish zerelete.

LXXXVI.

On, on and on, he sped, till suddenly,
  With deafening shock, the bay, a sea of flame,
Flash'd full in view! He turn'd in fright to flee,
  Wild as a murderer hearing his own name!
    He thought of death, of hell, with quivering
      frame!
He thought his deeds had helpt inflame their ire,
  Till all the Thunders seem'd to bellow —
    "Shame!"
And Winds hiss'd, hooting on, and would not tire —
" A curse to self and all! and all the world on fire!"

LXXXVII.

He ran, and ran, as tho' to outstrip thought!
  Yet only fann'd its fuel, red to white!
And made the dogs bark louder, tho' for naught.

He whirl'd aface a window where was light.
  Its beams suggested hope! he curst the sight:
And turning, plung'd far into kindred dark:
  But as he dash'd along, with frenzied might,
Upon the pavement fell a trembling spark:
He crush'd it with his heel, and sought the broader
    park.

LXXXVIII.

Half way across, his passion's hot-tooth'd flames
  Freeze, icy blades! A fearful shriek cuts through
The fitful surges of the storm! and shames
  The sever'd thunder! Lanterns loom in view!
  And sly police, assured, at last, of clew
From quick steps where the poor boy hies from fear.
  Then oh, how swift through lawn and lane he
    flew,
Till all was gloom again! when, drench'd and drear,
He hid beneath a shed to wait till dawn draw near.

LXXXIX.

And last it does come! From his crimson couch,
  The Sun draws back the curtains of the East;
While stealthy shades, through fen and forest crouch;
  Or, 'scaping westward, leave the world releast
  From dismal spells that still'd the man and beast.
Winds, wide, aroused, shake up each rustling wood,
  As tho' they whisper'd — " Wake, your thralldom's
    ceast!"
And birds, that dream'd all night of morning mood,
  Chase the faint stars, or find them flown with glee
    renew'd.

XC.

Soon, o'er the high hills lifts the sovereign crown,
   When, gayly garb'd in homage of their king,
The dew-bright Groves and Grasses bend low down,
   Then yield their midnight gains to vapory wing.
   Pleased with the stores of glittering wealth, they bring,
Their prince speaks festive day! whence sounds of praise
   And fragrant incense float: and sweet bells ring
Of hour, for men to muse, 'mid prayerful lays,
Of that bright morn when comes the Prince of all the Days!

XCI.

Ay, ay He comes, after all storm and rain,
   When glory gilds above the last dim night,
When peace fills back the last faint sigh of pain,
   He comes, He comes to usher endless light!
   Wake up, oh Earth! E'en now, half led by sight,
Behold! and track the tempest by the rose!
   And through the wake of war, the way of right!
Behold! while each fresh breath of morning blows,
How sweet, how beauteous life beneath the darkness grows!

XCII.

But he, whose night had pass'd so drearily,
   For whom the wise Winds whisper'd in their round,
For whom the brisk birds chirpt so cheerily,

For whom the bright sun up the heavens wound,
Till brave work bustled by, with praiseful sound,
Old men moved lightly, and glad children leapt,
Amort to hope and happiness profound,
Lull'd to long weary dreams while tired storms wept,
Stretch'd on the chill, damp ground all through the dawning slept.

XCIII.

At length, a farmer, stranger to the throng,
Happening to spy the boy, through curious ken,
Approach'd: and rousing him, with accents strong,
Cried:—"My young run-a-way, I've caught you then?
Good care I'll take you do not run again!—
Ho! cartman! go you toward the station now?—
I wish to move a sick boy, out this pen.—
You've place enough for us. I'll show you how—
Put me here, on the seat, and him there, by the plow!"

MI.

SUMMER had come; and with too heated Suns
Whose lazy pace allow'd lax Nature's strength
In whim to bud, ere wasting for the grain,
Came long vacation for the college lad.
How gladly shunn'd he, in the poet's room,
Maternal art, with brisk anxiety,
Fain' forcing on the museful student-mood,
On misanthropic seeming of soul-thought,
Picnics, tea-parties, and too gushing girls!
And how inspiring there the old man's words!
There is a time when youth must pass those gates,
The dismal passages 'neath castle walls,
That lead up from the park where childhood sports
To hall wherein the chieftain meets his clan.
If long the way, if dark, then strongly rear'd
Those fortress walls of his inheritance.
Nigh such a change in life, rung out this voice,
Like some wise counsellor's to the youthful knight;
"Yield not thy soul to Earth; nor body yet
To Heaven; become not libertine, nor monk;
Strip not, for naked shame, Heaven's virgin soul;
Nor shroud warm veins to mourn a lying death;
One thing thy birthright bids thee be, a man!"

POEM THIRD.

DOUBTING.

I.

FATE gave me feelings all my own,
And dreams that others had not known,
And doom'd me thence to dwell alone.
Who cares for me in all the street?
Away, away to drear retreat,
Along the gloom that throngs through all,
I feel the damp and mouldering wall,
And up the slimy stairway crawl.
I reach my home, an attic high,
Wherein I weep, and watch the sky,
And in my melancholy ply
Long day, long night, and try to earn
The strength and sphere for which I yearn,
With mouth to fill, and mind to learn.
I'd till, to reap from sweating brain,
Much thought, but, slight with all my pain,
It needs calm nature's sun and rain.
Whate'er I gain I'd sow again,
But who can tell me how or when
One cultures self for grateful men.

II.

I have a hope, of good to see
Past towering gates of mystery,
If men would trust the key to me.
I have a hope, earth's poor might find,
Behind those walls, a future kind
Where none are weak, and none can bind:
And yet, I fear, few let one be
The full design of destiny,
Unless install'd by royalty:
The common eye adjusts its glass
With larger lens to self, alas!
And small and far seem all who pass.
There's something in ordaining grace,
That priest and prince of every race
Have sought through mystic lines to trace,
Something behind the sword and gown,
Power apostolic, handed down:
There are no wise men to the clown:
The royal mind, in tent or town,
Owes generous genius for its crown.

III.

The whole I do, it is no use,
The while this devil's cur, abuse,
Is ever barking at one's heel,
Provoking sighs, he should conceal,
And tripping love until it reel.
To-day I ought to have withstood:
My aim, oh! was it not for good?
Why did I meet the man I hate?

Why did he stand there, in his state,
Smirk at me, and commiserate? —
For anger? — is that ever wise?
Let nature speak, spite all disguise,
That still will blush to feel it rise.

IV.

The heart's a heavenly harp when strung
For harmony of thought and tongue
These froward lines of life among.
What rallying charm where tune is one!
But how repelling, such undone!
Too oft, in sad comparison,
Its tones relaxt chord not with others;
How can one hope to blend with brothers
When every nerve, in wildest might,
Is strain'd to equal passion's hight?
Alas! how jars the air we smite!
How gentle faces shrink away!
"Far better than the wild man's lay,
Than discord rousing discord aye,
His rival mild, tho' wrong!" they say:
And so they shun one, night and day.
Oh God! for skill that comes of prayer,
To hear thy key-note everywhere,
Of love, with melody so rare,
It leaves no ear for harsh tone there.

V.

Perhaps, for more self-confidence,
These men about me, judging thence,
Might yield my thought more reverence.

I think who do good work should feel
There's naught enthroned to make right kneel.
One may have swayful temperament,
Or may look wisely, or be sent
With deeper worth not lightly seen ;
The beasts that kick at such a mien,
They must be whipt from their disdain ;
When broken once, they'll mind the rein.
No power for Worth awaiting place
Till deed outdo untried disgrace.
Awake my Soul! wake every power
Of prose, or rhyme, and from this hour
Let Rest grow zealous! Sleep watch clad!
Peace turn a pest! Contentment mad!
And slander'd Skill, with well dealt stroke,
Conquer its hope — to conquer hope!
Come wounds! Come jeers! where were they miss'd
By one who sought the noblest list?
Zeal ne'er did sigh, but some drone hiss'd :
" Be dunce with me or egotist!"
Wise World! that better due you grudge us,
Years hence, you'll better understand!
If we work out the good, so judge us!
If ill, time then to heat the brand!

VI.

This home of mine, it is a place,
More dainty doubts might deem disgrace,
But not its hungry populace.
For earth is small, and few can find
The gold to gild the life assign'd ;
And place is true, and few maintain

More splendid state than they can gain.
At first, I bore a wondering mien,
And oft did mourn when I had seen
How man could boast yet be obscene;
But oh! I feel, as days wear on,
Vice grown familiar grows less wan:
The sting of sin wears blunt anon:
One learns to learn, with so small fear,
That love and life do not appear
Full-wedded, in this lower sphere.

VII.

At times the door will shake with knock
That numbs the air! I breathe — a shock!
I dare not stay, nor dare I go
To welcome in the drunken foe.
Again, there sounds a shriller voice:
I shudder, tho' secure by choice:
Ideals all unseen by friends,
The blaze that comes from holy ends,
All lure of baser lust transcends.

VIII.

Sometimes, at midnight's moody hour,
Mysterious movements overpower.
I saunter out, explore the hall,
Afraid of each, but daring all:
'Twere death to speak, yet would I call:
I linger long, tho' throbbing heart
Repeat, — "Depart! depart! depart!"
Well fearful lest, if fear shall fill,
Insanity, the glee of ill,

Unbend the bent of wiser will.
When turn'd, at length, from all before,
Swift from beneath me flies the floor;
And swift, behind is barr'd the door,
As tho' pursuing monsters ran
To scath the spirit, and the man.

IX.

Ah! sad is life alone, alone,
Too sad when Thoughts, once proud to roam,
Chided and whipt, come mourning home
With their young ardor overthrown!
There was a time when, brave and bare,
The little hands, so soft and spare,
Claspt all, and hoped that love was there;
Ungloved by fear, claspt everything,
With every rose to grasp a sting,
Then shrank to shelter suffering.
And what are now desires about?
Oh! they have turn'd from deed, to doubt:
They work within, if not without:
Oh! they have turn'd, from world of pain,
To that still world within the brain,
Of fancy forming mead and main.
Back driven from the sunlight sought
They search through self!— ah! thence have caught
Some things, with prime perfection fraught,
There mirror'd 'mid mild wells of thought.
I sometimes think — it may not please —
Restless of ill, it would appease,
Imagination's a disease;

All deepest truths of thoughtful art,
From quick throes of an injured heart,
In fever to ply out a dart.

X.

They call me morbid, — if that be
A hate of wrong in world and me,
Love only for unseen ideal,
And sadness not to find it real,
Welcome the name, whoe'er has given:
Earth's titles cannot bias Heaven.
Her normal moods may sink and swell,
At one with a tide that bears to Hell;
Maturity — no flush decoys,
Shown spotless for too ardent boys —
Be ashes where Heaven's fire is spent,
Calm, cold, accursed, and content.

XI.

Accepting need, to dwell alone,
Has one robb'd right, who shields his own?
I've, too, deem'd reticence a vice,
And to the thought been sacrifice.
My life, I gave men, tho' each nerve
Strung for such blows, as mean men serve,
Twangled, for strain that might deserve
To be the seventh Hell's harbinger!
My fate, well mark'd, thought I, 'll deter
Like vengeance on like sufferer.
Starting to plan some doubtful scheme,
"Well frank," I cried, "with self the theme,
Fools gibber, goblins of the dream,

But wise men, for encouragement,
May hear what shall make confident."
'Twas truth: alas a world-wide tale!
Not all can conquer without mail:
What spurs the strong may stab the frail.

XII.

To restless limbs, calm sleep were sweet:
Who cannot sleep may scan the street
To search for watchmen in their beat —
Slow dusky forms, with echoing feet —
I stretch far out, I gaze far round:
'Tis strange to hear no human sound! —
And be so distant from the ground!
I fancy I am thrown adown,
Think how the news will stir the town: —
"A youth was found stone dead, they say;"
"Ah yes, I heard, good day: good day." —
Ho! ho! what now? why did I start,
The window slam, with blinds apart?
This mirror mocks! a queer grimace! —
Men differ slightly in the face! —
And how might this a madman grace? —
Oh God! — but ah! before I kneel'd
I found, I felt that stronger shield,
Where'er Woe bids the spirit yield.

XIII.

How near proud Reason's regency,
That wild Charybdis-craving sea,
That Malstrom of insanity!
We wander o'er the misty strand:

There swells the surf; here stops the land:
Smooth are the waters; soft the sand:
"Prude sister Sense," we cry, "away!"
We wade the surge! we feel the spray!
We leap!— and God prolongs our day!
Ah! Holy Wisdom, if Thou be
The Logos from the Sacred Three
Whom not to know is misery;
And if the wise in Heaven dwell,
The unwise then— but who can tell?
May madness be the mood of Hell?
Where He who ruleth, ruleth well?
If fiends with their accursed breath
Can make to tremble lungs of death,
And into fever'd heat can fan
A life, for every wish of man,
A life, whose every wish is pain,
No world to give, no limb to gain
The worldly thing to satisfy,
For which all wish is train'd to vie,
And so, a worm that cannot die,
A burning in a quenchless fire,
An endless life naught save desire, —
If then, the Passions pester'd sore
By Passions' lust indulged no more,
And wrong remember'd o'er and o'er,
Upspring, and, rousing all reserve
Oust Reason, from command of nerve,
What state can anarchy preserve?
What state?— Oh Christ, I see it rife!
And why thy Power, from typic strife,
Did cast out devils in this life!

XIV.

Afaint and far, the midnight bell,
And watchman's cry! With every knell
Does Conscience speak: "For Heaven or Hell,
One day toward death! and is all well?"—
How uselessly, through wanton ways,
Men bow and pass these stranger Days;
So wrecks, that in an ocean lave,
Now up, now plunged beneath a wave,
Steer not, one sinking soul to save.
But life!—has life no nobler state
Than shifting thus to drift of fate?
Has man no more than hulk to feel
The lurch of surge along the keel?
Tho' course, oft lightly turn'd about,
Be veer'd away from stronger doubt,
Come all his motives from without?
Are there no powers of deed within,
The mind's machinery to win,
A source of strife, a source of sin?
Moves not the soul when low depths thrill,
An image of perfection still,
And God-like by creative will?
Or yields not Heaven some gleams to thought,
Some hopes by Spirit-whispers brought
To outspeak fears the storms have taught,
Till holy lights far lands reveal
To guide the way of wavering zeal
To that which mists no more conceal?

XV.

Much have I read, how deep the vale
Whence some have heard high Fortune hail,
Who, seizing sword and shield and mail,
Have found the power to wound the wrong,
To dash aside its lances long,
And press between its yielding throng;
Till, helmet bright by brunt so vast,
Wrapt Wonder linger'd where they pass'd,
And older Glory shunn'd the last.
Anon they stood above the throng,
Immortal as the woe of wrong,
The light and lure of all the strong:
There peace with power forever dwells:
A grateful world their story tells:
Whoe'er repels, all love refels:
And victory swells unenvied bells.

XVI.

Yes, all made men are self-made men;
We ask too much of friendship then:
The soul's best impulse, in the end,
Is evermore the soul's best friend.
Truth whisper'd only to our spirit,
Why mourn, tho' none beside us hear it?
With honor craved, let one be strong
For worth to make dishonor wrong:
Or if a sceptre, let one find
A task befitting sovereign mind.
No low ambition they work out
Who seek, with energy devout,

A deed to match God's gift of will,
With thankful heart, remembering still
That shallow depths are first to fill,
And want is not yet stored with ill.

XVII.

While men with self are satisfied,
The things that are, they must abide:
And but to-day what is is best:
To-morrow all must move for rest.
Yet ne'er o'er darkness had begun
One truth its shining course to run
But snakes crawl'd out to hiss the sun:
"Who's seen the like? have you? have you?"—
"No never, no, my whole life through!"—
"A plague to Job! it will not do!"—
Why should men greet with reverence,
A thought beyond experience?
It were a libel on their sense!
Lo! in Earth's bigot brotherhood,
The fools alone are understood:
And only stupid people good.
But while the rest are dozing late,
Genius, quick-sighted for her fate,
Will wonder, wish, and work, and wait:
Her aim, far fixt for looming schemes,
Apart from those the world esteems:—
Else would she know but common themes:—
We are not always curst, when sent
By throes of nature's discontent
To abnormal development:
We are not curst till we consent.

The Faiths that die, first cease to dare.
Best, if one beacon guide life there,
Snatch hope from talons of despair,
And welcome flight with fancies fair.
In the vague light of ages old,
The poets were the first who told
The truths to make late logic bold.

XVIII.

If unveil'd vision could divine
The road that winds this mount of Time,
And view, but once, in clear outline,
The glory at the summit's prime;
And gaze below where foul mists creep
Along black waters of the deep,
Note slippery stones to trip the feet,
And crags to crush the indiscreet,
How closely would one watch and tread
The narrow, narrow path ahead!
But oh! should he discover trace
Of one supremely dangerous place,
Through thought of others in the race,
He might forget himself, and try,
Spite plains too wide, and hills too high,
To sound alarm with warning cry.
What tho' the Earth should deem him fool,
Fanatic, fiend, Chimera's tool!
Or hang to tree for witchery!
If body but swung o'er the danger,
Sweet dreams might date from deed of grace.
Corpses, there are, can tell the stranger
What might have flush'd o'er living face.

Better Isaiah sawn in two
Than life complete with nought to do
But lounge a useless journey through.

XIX.

Woe me! I boast, but cannot be!
I may work words, whine out a plea
Capricious as all misery,
What then? — can screaming scare off pain?
Only a rattle of restless brain,
What do rhymes buy? whence comes their gain?
There is no gain to earth but gold:
All bright paths hold but a bruted fold.
Each jingles his jewels to bob and beck,
Like a bull with a bell bound over his neck.
With mob and snob, how can it vie,
A poet's protest to the lie?
Like children caught in pastures lone,
Truth's noblest forms, to beasts unknown,
Are gored and trampled and left to moan.
I search for gold: 'tis full noon-time:
And only those who try to climb
Can know how far these hights of rhyme:
Too slow I go who wait for bread:
Too hard my task: my strength is sped:
My health is gone: I shall be dead:
And leave all life's report unsaid.

XX.

What can I do? — compared with me
The slaves I once did think to free
Are kings! These chains to liberty

In one's own conscience clamp, to pest
Who would, but dare not, do his best,
While Truth falls dazzled by renown,
Or Hunger fawns to gilded crown.
What can I do? What have I done?
Oh God! where, where is good begun?—
With charity and wisdom one,
God — He may leave the too self-wise
To rear for self both soil and skies,
To fume defects, like fogs that rise
From ill-drain'd pools, and shade for lies
All boasted visions one may trust:
A man, thus blind, may be unjust;
Where he, descrying forms at bay,
Cries down vague lions in the way,
The keener glance of healthy sight
May find but safest paths to right.
A man who hears not well may fear
The restless rumbling of his ear,
His own diseased and faithless ear,
And dream that strife is marshaling.
For Prejudice in everything
Conjures what worst is rivaling.

XXI.

Why should I gaze, to blame the earth,
When I am woe, and it is mirth?
These men, they live, to joke and dance,
To feast and sing and sport at chance,
In happy homes, all hush'd from strife,
To love and rest with child and wife;
While I, like quack physician trying

Poisons on self, apart am lying,
Martyr to what needs not the dying!—
What scouts a sickly man's idea,
Too well to test his panacea!
Oh! can there be a wisdom whence
Not through another's say or sense,
But through their own experience
Men learn the space 'twixt earth and sky?
What folly then moves such as I!
Wild wish is mine, too long pursued:
I follow, but to worsen feud,
A phantom; or earth can't be righted.
Come good by other course incited.
When into doubtful paths they stray,
The wise turn back: they're fools that stay,
Consistent — for that title lacks,
Where wisdom grows and change attacks,
Consistent — monomaniacs!

XXII.

Grand it is new life to borrow,
Like a Spirit dead to sorrow,
Dead to all Earth's dread to-morrow,
And, awake to realm of laughter,
Rise from grief before and after.
Hail to wit, the wine is bringing!
Hail to song from sadness winging!
Music hail! when, down from ceiling,
Bright as heaven where stars are wheeling,
Echoes bound to earth, there dealing
Daze and dance to sight and feeling!
When such joyous moments coy us,
Why should graver thoughts annoy us!

On the dance! But ah! this dancing! —
It were better if entrancing
From the soul-life were appealing
'Mid the blaze and buzz and wheeling,
And no lower range of feeling!
When her best ideals lure her,
Only then can forms assure her
That the soul is growing purer.
How can pride of sense or spirit,
For the public eyes that leer it,
Be embraced and never sneer it?
Press'd to breast and never fear it? —
Pugh! — just there the inn-maids head them
Spite pa's debts, to deck and wed them!

Back to music! Ah! the music
Seems all holy when we muse it!
Surely woe could never use it!
All our life we start and wonder
What the blunder in this under
World woke Heaven to voice of thunder —
But 'tis there! — and strong to sunder
Like the storms that gather madly
Round the days that dawn all gladly,
'Twixt the heart and heavens, sadly
Steal on holy harmonies
Thoughts from where no music is.

Back to feast! Hurrah! they cheer it!
Here's to health! — What! don't they hear it?
Here's to health! — What! dare they jeer it?
Lo! they tremble! do they fear it?

Hark!—My soul!—a man has tumbled!—
There's a beast! and God is humbled!—
Weeps a wife that ne'er is sleeping!
Children, her thin hands are keeping!—
Waits a grave where none are weeping!

Back from Earth! There's no fruit in it
Fit to peel! When you begin it,
Curst, you find a worm within it!—
Fiend away! Who'll hold?—I never—
That a devil's hoof should ever
Roil all springs for faint endeavor!
'Tis our eye that sees no season:
'Tis our ear that heeds no reason:
'Tis our touch turns joy to treason,
Joy, no, never meant to curse us,
But design'd to nerve and nurse us.
Oh for Right to reimburse us,
Dawning for such day above all,
Heaven should guide, where good could love
  all!

XXIII.

Sad from self-satiety,
Why should one shun society?
Ah there awake, from dark dejection,
Those dismal dreams of introspection!
There, 'mid the tramp of multitudes,
God too communes through many moods,
For much that were not understood
Where self with self alone did brood.
And better idiot, 'stride a chair,

Dreaming a kingdom out of air,
With stock-still statues for hussars,
With scarfs of knighthood but the scars
Deep-whipt across a bleeding back,
Than be a man whose soul must lack
The train that waits on Friendship's throne,
For manhood's kingship, Love alone.

XXIV.

Blest Love, it reigns in Heavenly hight:
It reigns on earth: but mark its might!—
I'd have no friend, in dark or light,
Whose love embraced not love of right.
Life's changeful times need righteous mood
To judge of mien not understood
By faith remembering former good,
Faith man as well as God demands
From soul that nearest to him stands.
Full oft one's doubt or danger could
Express no purpose, if it would,
Yet then one likes to be thought good?
And oft there comes a need of rest,
But earth is like a sick bird's nest,
All beaks of fellows at one's breast.
Strange cure!—yet 'tis an old complaint—
Much, much of love, when only faint,
Is peckt to death to make a saint.

XXV.

Know! in the soul's a deal of yearning
That silent thought is slowly turning
To deepest and to highest learning,

That can't play mistress to a Why!
Life, like the sailor, steers to sky,
If mists, offscourings of the sea,
Conceal the brightness on the lea,
It fails in reckoning, may be;
Then ye of little faith, oh why
Crowd ye, like passengers who fly
In fright to captain, but to ply
A failure, miracle, or lie?

XXVI.

Ah! in our good society
Lies are a link to sympathy!
And hearts with widest difference
Tickled and one at touch of sense!
Yet all true love, it loves the soul,
And naught more lovely can control
Than Nature frank itself to dole.
Let foe desert such, friendship dwells,
Nor fears in truth, behind false spells,
What saddens sight of beaus and belles.
I've seen a man and maid, to-day,
Splashing each other's eyes with spray:
Enough had he, from depth obscene,
To please my lady's wistful mien,
Not vicious all, but proud I ween
Of vice the patron, wide of eyes
For him on whom the shamed relies —
Lust has such luscious flatteries!
And wit it wakes, a dash of danger
With one who's in the mart, a ranger!
Of spice it smacks, while he's a stranger,

While he's a knave and she's a flirt,
And if they marry, for dessert
Will find life's game, dish'd up in dirt!

XXVII.

Who culls the grain of friendship knows
There's little natural now that grows,
There's little yield except of stalk,
A hot-house flowering of talk
From hot-house friendship, with the root
So little in the soul, 'twill suit
Quite well to have so little fruit.
The usual weed's a gossip-shoot,
The toadstool from what's rotten there.
A gossip is a scavenger
Of other people's character,
And to a man of finer sense,
Brought up with care in purer air,
Disgusting are the sediments.

XXVIII.

They scarcely let one rest in bed,
With all their whispers round him sped, —
Of stupid born and sparely bred.
Weak tribunes of strong character,
Too snuggish friends, I do aver,
Throng every mart, and boast an ear
Well hugg'd against the heart, to hear
Each secret lull and throbbing dear.
Why silent not of things unknown?
Why force, by tales one cannot own,
To leave too blusterous love alone?

Rather than figure as the fool
I could inoculate, nor pule,
The chronic kicking of the mule!
Play owl, night's nightmare, with a toot
Selfish enough to scandal brute!
And rouse one universal hoot!
Ay, Earth, it is so full of fangs,
To save myself from probe and pangs,
I've shrunk again from its harangues,
In garret here, like Death in clouds,
Forever grateful there are shrouds
Hide worms beneath that coil'd and crost
From Heaven, half Heaven from what is lost.

XXIX.

Yet, 'tis not wholly misery
To be bereft of sympathy!
Perchance, a wise Omnipotence
Discloses surface difference
For unity in deeper sense.
There is a life below this strife
That feels the tender infancy
Of something grander yet to be.
There winds do whisper wish and speech,
And shades and shapes have reveries each
That guide Interpretation, driven
By prophecy, in ecstasy
To match pure moods of Earth with Heaven.
Perchance, when forced to gaze above
For life's completed boon of love,
Glimpses appear of what should be,
Till God who must for aye decree

Presence to those in sympathy
Trails robes of Truth to yearning hours,
Lighting to right, and luring powers.

XXX.

Of late, when I am all alone,
I pause, and bend before the throne
Of my delight, Philosophy!
A page of her bright train am I!
With eager soul, but patient eye,
I hie to every moving thing,
Thence to report of life the spring!
I fancy earth as fire — or air —
Or mind itself, so conjuring there :
I press against the window pane,
Ask — feels the nerve? or feels the brain?
What spans this space 'twixt sense and soul?
Faith? or the Absolute? or whole
From flow and ebb of thoughts that roll? —
Am I who muse eternally,
Without responsibility,
The vagrant wave of some vast sea?
Or am I all ; and earth a lie?
And nothing better past the sky?
These things about not what they seem?
And even life itself a dream? —
Comes, truth, I seek through reason clear?
Or does short sight, with organs blear,
See all things falsely looming here?
Then flashes right, like lightning glance?
Or dawns it o'er some dozy trance? —
Shall one know more when earth is done?

Reach misery? or oblivion?
Or through some mystic, spiral way,
Mount Babel bright to bliss for aye?—

XXXI.

Hold! Logic labors but to spy
What those who gaze with scrutiny
Detect as ancient heresy!
Does Church or State then speak the right?
Or is it better found by sight
Of conscience? or of laws that bless?
Or noblest wish? or happiness?
When started once in plainer ways,
The path, it winds amid a maze
Where things of hate wake wish unjust,
And naught! oh! naught is left to trust!
Then why search I save what is nigh?
These earthly eyes can never spy
Above where God lifts up the sky!

XXXII.

Ah! He who rules the sky rules dell!
Whate'er I doubt, I know full well
Who made the soul, must it impel;
And, tho' the way were black as Hell,
He moved to truth, who could but feel
His pathway true to true ideal.
When sweet and ceaseless calls appeal,
One cannot, dare not turn away.
What tho' the victory long delay!
A power courageous in the fray
To rattle rhymes, or beat a drum,

May rouse up spirit by the hum, —
That spirit for the right at war
The whole this life is given for! —
Yes! there is truth, I oft have thought,
One finds when he has only sought!

XXXIII.

Alas! but still desire will sink,
A mort of misery to think
'Tis now full nigh six thousand years
Since Lamech rhymed away his fears,
And men have search'd all earth about
Nor is there yet one less of doubt.
Oh what can later poet say
That he has found to aid the way?
Or how a later poet know
If good or ill have made him so?
Would God! some eye to scan the whole
Could but reveal what lures the soul,
With power that self cannot control,
Through these long days and sleepless nights,
So weary, weary from delights!
Why should a sense that shrinks from sight
Press out, to push itself in light,
A target bright for baser blight?
Where all things one can hope are good,
All gleams of individual mood,
Are flouted, or misunderstood?
I'd not wink greatness, if I could : —
Alive, a wonder-animal
Poked up by all things rational,
Barr'd back from truth by scrutiny,

From love by inequality:—
When dead, with bones dress'd out to be
The puppet of biography,
Forced now to dance too high, too low,
Too blest for friend, too base for foe
To please the men who make him go;
For ill with good immortal years,
That ill the humbler never fears
From lands beyond this vale of tears.
Ye fools, with faith in fame, relent!
Ah! this was never what they meant,
Those men of truth whose footsteps went
Through life that was one long ascent,
They looked beyond a monument!

XXXIV.

My mind seem'd wild from wilder'd thought.
I paced the stilly night, and sought
Rest from the rest about, above,
Something to teach me more of love.
I reach'd a church, with open door,
Whence strains along the air did pour,
The air that trembled, as it bore
This sacred sound of holy lore:

XXXV.

"God of Heaven, and man of manger,
Jesus, heed the need of stranger,
Wander'd far in way of danger,
   Wise no longer where to flee.
Holy Source of love and learning,
Hear a soul whose doubt is yearning,
From despair and anguish turning,
   Turning only unto Thee.

"Not regarding means or measure,
  I have sought through pain and pleasure,
  What the world can give to treasure,
    But alas! all fail to be,
  By the deep love of Thy mission,
  By the deeds for high ambition,
  By the gains of full fruition,
    Aught that Thou dost promise me.

"From my guilt and from pollution
  I have wrought for restitution
  Through the skill of resolution,
    All my will proves false to me.
  Far beyond my best endeavor
  Peace and pardon find I never,
  Never love and right together:
    Thou hast promised liberty.

"Past the methods and the mazes
  That the search of science dazes,
  Past the knowledge and the praises
    That the earth can give to me,
  From the farthest hights of learning,
  My desires must still be turning
  Toward the stars forever burning,
    Heaven and immortality.

"What can faith do?—Lord, I feel it:
  Bible, History, Thought reveal it:
  Christian lives and conscience seal it:—
    All true life begins with Thee!
  Base of wish and low of thinking,
  From each nobler duty shrinking,
  And with strength impair'd and sinking,
    Where beside can sinner flee?

"What if heart can boast no feeling,
  Languid through its need of healing,

Fill'd with pride still, still concealing
  Self and self-made misery?
When my soul has seen Christ dying,
When has heard His prayer and sighing,
Oh, it feels that Love replying
  Lingers not for worth in me.

"Nay! with Thine, all love possesses!
Nay! with Thine, all truth progresses!
Nay! with Thine, all pure life blesses!
  Thou canst be all things in me!
Oh, take, Lord, my Heart's donation,
All I own, in each relation,
Only to Thy free salvation
  Would I longer dare to flee!"

XXXVI.

Scarce into silence sank the song,
Before came forth, in accents strong,
That calmed the rustling of the throng
As words of "peace!" above the sea
When hush'd the troubled Galilee,
A text! —— and I, who stood there hearing,
I too felt calmness come to fearing,
A depth of peace reflecting of devotion
As heaven from lake where lingers no commotion:
And like to voyager with memory
Still fresh to moods that mused a peaceful sea,
Does that then heard and felt remain to me.

XXXVII.

"'The Truth — The Truth shall make you free!' Our souls
  Feel conscious of subjection. Throned o'er act
And wish, they feel a Power to punish them

And prompt obedience. Men name this Power
In varied terms — their conscience, their ideal:
All hold it Truth, a Truth revealing laws
For nature, circumstance and destiny:
And, by as much as few live true to it,
By so much few can fail to feel it chide.
To all who would escape it it is proved,
By Omnipresence, not produced by self's
Reluctant will; and, by its claims on love,
Akin to personal authority
With source no fancy, nor abstract idea,
But concrete life altho' a Spirit life.
And when one man of holy deed declares
Himself the King of Kings, the Spirit's Lord,
'I am the Truth!' why should Faith doubt the word?
If miracles and prophecies sustain'd,
If progress of the years confirm the claim,
Seems Truth in Person strange? Has earth no need,
No deep desire for one to incarnate
This spiritual sway, that He be model?
And teach pure laws inspired to guide toward right?
And in the soul incite what germinates,
And grows, and bears fruit for the Spirit's life?
Oh ye! with conscience sad for thought or deed,
If sadness do result from Power Divine,
Think not without deep change to 'scape the state
That He ordains. Such effort fails. The laws
Of Truth but work your wrath: all strife to spite
But works your hatred, like to rebel's strife
That but makes clear a king's authority.
The Truth can never change. 'Tis ye must change
To love its rightful rule. Ay, once love Truth,
All duty shall be freedom. See this Truth,
Through Truth Incarnate dying on the cross;
Learn thence how much of love there is in God;
Learn that from Him comes all to make life blest;
E'en while you learn, instinct as nature, Love
Shall follow Him, the while His Spirit prompts

And cause pure deeds, obedient to each law
Without this goading consciousness of sin!
Would you be free, incarnate Truth in self,
His Spirit of all Truth, Heaven cannot bind!

" Reach freedom thus for Nature in desires.
Oh! have you never felt that heart of life
Which, through the unseen arteries and veins
Of Spiritual Being, still propels
An Omnipresent ebb and flow of Love? —
Desires that search far off in thoughts, that steal
Stillness from sleep, and rest from reverie? —
The lonely wishes of the single soul,
Oppress'd from sense of sunder'd sympathy,
Struggling to meet the universal Whole? —
Dream not to sate these wants by earthly gains!
Impell'd to such, the boy would be a man;
Maids blush for maidenhood; and lovers kneel;
Then fiercely strive for wealth! and power! and fame!
Aiming at fullness still beyond their reach,
Till wasted strength shrinks back infirm of zeal,
Or holds all earth, to feel e'en that too small,
All Alexander's pride but vanity!
For oh! Desire, it seeks the Infinite;
The life of nature, not the make of art;
To be at one with God, the Life of Truth! —
And need ye ask what Power can join to God? —
Ah His, who bore our sins that faith be free
From fear of justice and from doubt of love
And learn of character first blest above,
His Truth shall bring desire to liberty!

" Reach freedom thus for Nature's destined deeds.
Poor finite, frail and over-burden'd soul,
Be not abash'd of self. Truth shall succeed.
Here is a place where weakness, well confess'd,
Surrenders naught. Nay! nay! it chooses part
Where Pride could ne'er attain nobility!

Where Self kneels down, to rise, a royal priest
In the grand chancel of Humanity!
Before its shrine, there's no one, not the least,
But has his mission, station'd between Earth
And Heaven, half spirit, half mortality,
To take that loan of life receiv'd at birth, —
Its germ, its growth, and all its varied grain, —
And offer it, like to that greater Priest
Who offered more, a willing sacrifice
Upon that altar where this human soul
Is put to test of strife with Heaven-sent flames;
Then from experience, his lone legacy,
To cull tried relics of the Spirit's life,
Deep worth disclosed, and preservations grand
Of common things our use profaner slights;
And dower'd with these, before all earth to stand,
Sacred of self for what the self reveals,
Both victim and the seer, hushing Earth's fears.
And doubtful murmurs by sublime appeals
Taught through the language of life's work fulfill'd.
Oh ye! who crave faith, faith in what ye are,
No selfish wish need that be, if ye crave
No praise for frailties known, but shun afar
With equal dread false flatteries and frowns!
On! Onward still! God speed ye, restless souls!
Claim manhood's mission, clear acknowledgment
Of royal priesthood! honor for your truth!
And, with your own, the world's development!

"Live self! but not for self, remembering aye
For one, for all, the Truth brings liberty!
For self, free hearts, free hands; for others, charity!
It is no selfish bearing slights repute
In Godly consciousness of Truth ideal.
Still more and more do heirs of higher weal,
With lips to worldly blame and praises mute,
Love each in each the Truth that makes all free.
Ah! when men learn how Infinite that is,

And how diverse on earth its ministries,
There is a reverence here for word and deed;
If one but feel Truth gains the victory,
A soul contented, e'en though self may fail:
Or if one feel Lie thrives, still strong is faith
From love more Lord-like, while afar yet near,
Less than whole love, but more than interest,
Love that can waive a full complacency
In deference to the worth each may attain,
And thoughts of Christ, prompting to missions here
With help for all who need, and hope that shall be blest!"

XXXVIII.

Have I found faith? — The faith my life did covet
I deem shall come not all through thinking of it.
It may be, 'spite the monk's abstraction,
The consciousness of life is action,
And goodly grain is best reveal'd
Not far from harvest plain conceal'd,
But to the one who tills the field.
Ah, tho' I may still doubt, I know
Of prayer when Heavens do overflow
For showers of bliss, e'en though below.
And Words I read of truthful prime
That do not sound like words of Time,
In joy or sorrow all sublime.
And Love I watch that springs apace,
Through sun and storm alike to trace,
And all who live it grow in grace.

XXXIX.

Do these suffice? — I think, perchance,
That where these lines of Truth advance
Man has not right of ordinance.
Oh! if it be Experience
 Need rescue wish from negligence
In thought or deed, the long years hence
May prove all blows but benefit
From which wise Doubt learns to submit;
From which an unwise Trust in it,
While fails some low support of love,
Is slowly taught to look above.
Earth needs that lesson! I descry
Who glorify the Lord on high
Reveal His beauty through their own,
And purify the men who vie
Attracted by the God-like shown.

XL.

With soul not shown, too much of art
Is made for lips to fit the heart.
Not skill to chide another's pride
Shall make one wise or welcome guide.
Who best provokes to patient deed
First traces best his own first need.
Be his need great, and other's small,
He may be less yet more than all.
Nay all, perchance, have equal call
With ill to bear, and good to share,
 And, whether it be full or spare,
Some truth to show the Christ-like there.

Let then the Spirit's voice be heard,
Tho', like to warbled wish of bird,
Wise only through vague sounds of word,
The men who hear and turn to sky
I will believe, if love be nigh,
Are blest tho' heaving but a sigh.
Who wants to fill the earthly throne
Birth gave him not! far better own
One's self, and live one's self alone.

FA.

YOUNG was the village pastor for his work;
   And young his wooings of well worded thought,
Offer'd as some young beau presents his hand,
As tho' high color'd kids held first of rank
With her whose heart he'd lure to Paradise!
So far in life, study, meant most for brain,
And healthy growth, where heart fills out the last,
Had made him deal more cream from nice reviews
To sate a dainty taste, than solid meat
To nurture muscle for the strength of spirit.
With firmer faith in intellect that sketch'd
Harsh pictures of the soul, than in the soul
Which God had made an image of Himself,
He'd judged of men, as some men judge of flowers,
Not on the stalk, but pluck'd and press'd in books;
And deem'd the Catholic Church, not quite so broad
As one long ride his student days had known
'Twixt Andover and Princeton; and each school
Of Christian Charity, a place to prove
How all beside one's self are in the wrong.
So strange looks interchanged the while he read;
But some, recalling more love in late themes,
Nor yet one word less orthodox, surmised:—
Perchance, of late, he had been learning too.

POEM FOURTH.

LEARNING.

I.

ONCE, when I moved with those who walk'd by sight,
Came ways where Faith did pause to ask the right,
And words directing that made doubts increase,
So thwarting gains before, and present peace.
Sad then, and spirit spent, my life did veer,
As tho' to seek a clearer atmosphere,
From words of others, and from whims of mine,
To muse with Nature as with Thought Divine.

II.

'Mid woods and streams, my mood detected soon,
Dim-lighted by the reverent-minded Moon,
A temple, grown to shape where ivy-twined
Elms of wide trunk about far sides did wind
Of aisles, still sinking through a wild of naves;
Where years had bowed ambitious Architraves
For art complete, for roof through skill of Showers
Aye freshly fretted; and where fervent Flowers,
Fever'd and prostrate Nature's lord to greet,
Died for a dust of fragrance 'neath the feet.

III.

Anon, before me gleams a brook whose shore
I follow, flashing bright, — while Rays explore
Through tilt uplifted by the curious Wind —
A silver pavement, which rare jewels bind
To the long floor: and, motionless, each side,
All powerless to resist that lulling tide,
In arms of fondling Boughs do white Mists sleep
Like spirits chaste, trustful in Winds that sweep
With bugle-blast far off, and, drawing nigh,
Shall, on the morrow, waft them to the sky.

IV.

Meanwhile, the night is not devoid of sound:
Weird whispers prompt to thought of dreams around,
Mysterious moods of water wind and wing
Insect and beast, with long-drawn echoing,
Low-music, lingering lovingly along
The dew-drugg'd, perfume-drowsy air, as song
From bay-bound ships through dull November calms;
It sways the listening soul, as pensive psalms
That breathe mild melody from organ reeds,
Distilling gently while the strain proceeds,
Do fuse a sweetness through the atmosphere,
Our heaving breasts inhale, as well as hear.

V.

Calm as such chorals to the sense devout,
Came calmer nature to the course of doubt.
With gratitude for each cool touch of Air
That soothed the fever'd nerves, I rested there.

Amid my peace then, lo ! another came,
Whose soul-ful face woo'd from the soul a claim
Of sympathy complete, ere either spoke ;
But last, his voice reluctant reverie woke :

VI.

" Who does not love, 'mid shades and sounds like these
Most charming from suggested mysteries,
To throw aside, or strive to throw at least,
The learning of our Times, and cull a feast
From superstition ; and half envy freaks
With which mad Fancy fool'd those flighty Greeks ?
I know the Present has, in deeds, more right,
And more strength for the deeds ; still is its might
A boy's o'ergrown, — long legs and arms for strife,
But heart and lungs are weak. Deep wants of life
We value not. This home of Nature, grown
A common sight, our restless days disown :
And we forget that mysteries too are true ;
And we forget about the distant blue ;
And we forget about the silent pall ;
And Faith, the only thing that fathoms all.

VII.

" Better than no faith, faith that Æolus
Restrains the storms, so gentle Zephyrus
For his fair wife may tune, 'mid fragrant bowers,
These sweeter strains ; to praise, in such mild hours,
That lutes and boots and mantles scowls and showers
Of wilder winds are gone ; that no fierce rite,

No Furinalia could have claim'd such night
As parent; that no Thuellai affright,
No wench with vulture claws and serpent form
Crawls out the stream, or blusters through a storm;
That voices from Pelorus lure none here;
Narcissus boughs and wool do not appear
All matted o'er hag-faces, chuckling near
The grim fixt mask of Fate; that Naiades
Flit here; and, from fond homes, the Dryades
Chime sweetest cheer with serenading groups
Of truant minstrel-Hamadryad troops;
That Napææ wake chorus through the vale;
That eager Echo speeds her flight to hail
The long array of Oread choirs, whence quiver
The mountain-answers to the sea and river.

VIII.

"Better than no faith, faith that would not doubt
That Graces and frail Hours trip about
With Fauns, and jolly rustic retinue
Of Bacchus; or, just as the carvers drew
Round Pyrrhus' agate, on some greener spot,
Join'd hand in hand, all other cares forgot —
The scrolls and wands and masks and marks of
  craft,
And merry o'er a fresh Castalian draft,
With tongue and tread, the sacred Nine aspire
To vie with zest of Cynthius' nervous lyre,
While, ruling all, the reeds of Syrinx play,
And blend accordant each else diverse lay."

IX.

He rose to go; and I, who, well pleased, heard,
Rose too and follow'd him. Without a word
We saunter far, like Pilgrims near the shrine
Of long sought mosque, who clip the thin-spun line
Of speech, and do not wish one other gree,
Than, in the soul, that sense of Deity.
At length, "Oft do I marvel," he began,
" At man and world, so wisely one of plan !
An atom changed, and vapory means might swarm
To dim these heavenly hues! yes, bury form
Till it seem'd dead deformity! outweigh
All sweet breath of the flowers! and muffle aye
This music, fit to charm anew who hears,
'Mid holy air, more music of more spheres !

X.

"And yet, all life's our own life ! Shapes, to see,
Loom not beyond the Sight's capacity !
And all life grows with us ! and keenest sense
May sate of much, for much indifference !
Full many a Will, whose effort can compress
In climax crowded for suggestiveness,
Like rays in focus, Truth's whole range to bless,
Might thankfully surrender half the sway
Well polish'd power can wield, to be the prey
Of things that thrill'd his youth, so these reveal
That beauty he discerns, but cannot feel !

XI.

"All beauty can lead upward those inclined
To its intent. The wise and holy find
This round horizon — not a peopling mist
Of whims embodied to the polytheist —
This round horizon, where such wonders mass,
A strange strong lens, like Claude Lorrain's, a glass
Condensing great thoughts of one God, to fit
Their comprehension. But Heaven must emit
New blaze, I fear, compared with which, sunlight
Shall seem but gray! as lightning it must smite!
Ere one faint spark shall cheer the sense of moles!
Of blind who turn their back on Heaven and goals
Above, who burrow Stygian mire of earth,
And tomb their souls from all that life is worth,
Its language to the spirit! Ah, dim Skies!
When shall some universal dawn arise;
Fill space, for once, with claims so vast that fear
Shall overwhelm each groveling purpose here,
All wills bent low, till, gazing toward the blue,
They cry, with Paul, 'What wilt Thou have me do?'

XII.

"Weak mortal men may all be priests! — high
    priests
Of Nature! who shall gather up from beasts,
And birds, and creeping things, and the dumb earth,
And senseless skies, else but a blank in dearth
Of sentiment, the germs of praise in each;
And, adding to their substance then a speech
Of soul, breathe from the truths that all record

A tale, a life of glory to the Lord.
Ah, such Shechinah can dwell with each heart,
Make all His shrine whence worship shall impart
Praise, praise to every scene of life and art!"

XIII.

Here, stealing silence from his final word,
I ask'd, in reverence for the thoughts I heard,
Who it might be that thus communed with me?—
"A man whose study is humanity,"
He answer'd. "Oft," said I, "one finds that name,
Humanity, an ill-disguising claim
Of those whose sense of human worthiness
Loves man not more, but only God the less.
Yours seems not so. I ween your scrutiny
For good seeks God and not humanity?"

XIV.

"Both," he replied; "deem you His coin a fraud?
Shall one not seek His stamp, to learn of God?
Shall one not search His image?—for I fear it,
They see but sense who search not for the Spirit!"
"Alas!" rejoin'd I, "Once my soul did dare
To seek Him thus; but found doubt only there.
All the small trust I have scarce bides a prayer.
Of man, thought grows mature but to grow sad;
And learns the more, the more to learn of bad."
"Are you quite sure," said he, "one could not add
That 'tis a morbid mood, bilious complaint
Frets, finding Earth no Heaven, nor man a saint?
I've known a healthy Faith gaze round the ring
To trace with joy some good in everything."

XV.

"Hearken!" continued he, "who treads this hill
May reach that place at which, with stronger will,
The Prince of Good withstood the Prince of Ill.
From yon high peaks, which touch Eternity,
Kingdoms of earth that were, and some to be,
Lie present to the eye of History."
"But," said I, shrinking back, "dwells Ill still here?"
"Yes," answer'd he, "well those who walk with fear;
But well repaid. Time comes, in lives of men,
When things, once tempting, do not tempt again."

XVI.

Thus speaking he advanced; myself meanwhile
With hesitation following. Far we file
Past brook and crag, till, opening from a dell,
Comes sudden precipice, adown which fell
A stream in silence, then thunder'd farewell
A thousand feet below! Huge mountains bow
In reverence beneath, rich-wreathed of brow,
And robed of shoulder with those legacies
Translated Summer drops from closing skies.
Glancing to vales beyond, I sought to recall
Place where I was. "Look!" said my Guide, "how small
The objects there! all men appear the same!
Not one can force his own peculiar claim
Up through so slight a distance! Trust to see,
When nearer Heaven, still more equality."

XVII.

Then added he, "What gain for thoughtful toil!
What harvests 'mid such stretch of sky and soil!
What food for wisdom in one nook alone!
Here, such a feast to feed new growth is strown,
That, like the slave who snuffs and waits the bone,
One culls all joy of thought ere he collects,
Skips the slow course, and has its throng'd effects!
Yet even now we pause not. Mark you rays
To right of those far peaks that merge in haze?
Then nigh, where looms a loftier mountain range,
As though a storm were still'd by peace so strange,
Or on the verge of strife reclined for slumber?
Where forms from clouds above, and without number,
Press onward with such vague solemnity,
And not, as near here, tripping merrily
To music of these swaying pines? — to-night
Scenes hidden yet by that range claim the sight;
We must move on and up:" — which saying, then
He forth began to climb, 'twere hard to pen
Through what long wastes of ledge and brake and fen.

XVIII.

But, on a high, broad cliff his quick pace ceast,
And thence, the while he points far toward the east,
I can descry, upon a greener field
Swept of the cumbering trees, — but half conceal'd
'Mid smoke and incense whiter than its own
Pure marble hue, — an altar; nor alone;

Soon, standing nigh, or knelt in reverent fear,
Do white-robed multitudes of priests appear.
Then, many people more ; all search a sign,
Some movement amid victims on the shrine ;
And, ever and anon, borne o'er the blast,
Do loftier fragments of deep praise float past,
Soft interrupted strains which beat the air
As tho' vibrations from the wings of prayer.
Just as I seek to learn the cause of all,
The smoke, grown dense, ascends, a darkening pall,
Unwrapping through successive folds, and spreads,
As Paripanou's tent, above the heads
Of the vast throng, past all foretoken'd size !
Thence upward carried, each fresh current vies
To sprawl its dingy wings along the skies,
Like that grand hypocritic drapery o'er
The pyre of dead Pompeii, rear'd of yore
By her fierce executioner, the grim
Vesuvius ! swift, like that, does it dim
All objects, save its own mass hovering
On high, here shading and there covering
The moon and struggling stars ! ere long it takes
New shapes ! Another blast of tempest shakes
Its length ! when sally forth foreboding forms,
Like thunder-clouds far grasping out in storms !
And then, as tho' a frame of life, they lower
Heaven-wide ! the limbs of some stupendous Power
Resting on air ! while Scrutiny would wait,
He slowly moves ! his mighty breasts inflate !
His giant fingers touch the yielding space !
"Watch !" cries my Guide, "watch well, and you
    shall trace

Creations new! bright surges, dark mirtlock,
And patals, where foul bands of Nardman flock,
Flow forth to fill the heavens! Brahma! again
I see thee ride above the Indian main,
Borne on thy lotus-car, while Truth began
To gild the dreams of youth and guide the man!

XIX.

" Ah thought was crystallized to make a world!
Be He the southern Kneph, or He who hurl'd,
'Mid frozen climes, the heat from Muspellheim
Into Ginnunga-gap, or He with prime
Efficient will discern'd 'mid twilight dim
Of Grecian lore, and many a prayerful hymn,
All nations feel a God, e'en through thick mist
Of Earth-fumed theory cannot resist
Suggested thoughts of One who doth sustain
And did create the universe. In vain
Immortals strive for rest, who have no vows
For that First Source, before whom Conscience bows
Conscious of wise and moral Governor.
Let Hindoo be our soul's interpreter
With proofs of God that Hell may be more sad.
With Siva to develop from the bad
And Vichnu savior join'd with Brahma, One,
A Parabrahma, union such as none
Can comprehend, as binds three Persian Powers,
As shifts for aye the dark Egyptian hours,
With three dejotas merged in Trimurti,
Where learn'd the soul this thought of Trinity?
Was He, whose name His chosen dared not trace,
One with Jehovah of another race

Which named Him not, who promised to redeem
A world from wretchedness, and wake a dream
Of peace with Heaven's full blessedness? Ah! who
With eyes and ears shall find naught that is true?
Amid the worst, some whiff of right has given
Fresh breath to Faith that totters on toward
    Heaven."

XX.

I look'd. The shape had vanish'd. Left behind
Is naught but smoke which now does gently wind
About the stars. Then, when these gleam amain
From the clear'd sky, he shows me, o'er the plain
Those obelisks, "the son of Mitres rears
To meet and match the rays of worshipt spheres.
Chaldee!" he sigh'd, "If stars be numberless
To man, has therefore God such feebleness?
Ye clove the sense of His Infinity,
To name each whit a god, in mockery!
Minerva sprang from Jove, but Jove survived.
Thy Vulcans struck for idols, Truth still thrived:
And shall thrive, till no priests, like thine, shall revel,
Belus! first incarnation of the devil!"

XXI.

While speaking, he had turn'd, and left that scene
For region rough with mounts. Past Mosses lean
And mourning Pines, from many an aspiring home
Fleet Torrents dash, excited but to foam.
More modest, in more quiet walks beneath,
Bright genial Springs succeed, 'mid grateful Heath,
Reflecting light from open skies above.

Nigh one, sweet to intoxicate to love,
" Behold you," said my Guide, " that glimmering nave
Form'd from the cragged arches of this cave?
'Tis carved with symbols the great magus gave.
Within, seven blazing dadgahs light his plan
To overthrow the power of Ahriman.
Well for his fame, that the wise seer found signs
So full of hope; could picture in such lines
That Zend Avesta lured the peoples' heart;
Show Mithras, not for aye, with threaten'd art,
In twilight time, preserving peace between
The white-mail'd Ormuzd and his foe obscene
Dark Ahriman, but crown'd where every spirit,
Named sinless from Tschinevad. should inherit
Unclouded realms of endless day, once more
Good only reigning supreme as of yore.

XXII.

"But Zoroaster was not last, nor first
To learn of life by which the world is curst.
Nay! name him Typhon, Loki, Moisasure,
Who does not ask, how long shall Ill endure?
Well welded locks and legal barriers
By which the best philanthropist avers
A worst distrust; the long lewd list of crimes
In lawyers' lore; the armies of all times,
With men so pleased to man them; Anarchy
That sweeps with waves of blood for misery
Where bayonets rear no breakers; Toil that schemes
For self, and stores another's; Rest that dreams
Of vice and wakes in vileness; Conscience, Care,

Disease, and Death ; — alike one record bear
To handling of an ill power gone before,
With tampering clear to all, but clear the more
To those who are most keen to spy the right;
Where blear eyes blink, but health detects the blight."

XXIII.

The cave, pass'd by, shoots through thick-wooded path,
Like furnace fires at gloaming, many a shaft
Of light which routs the perils of the way
And haunts uncertain Night with ghosts of Day.
But woods and rays, at length, give place to plain
From which I gaze up toward the mounts again.
There do I note, upon a summit tall,
Some stealthy Mists. Anon, they seem to crawl
Along the hights, and lengthen out, and show
They are but first of others, gathering so.
These soon close up behind them, with low hum,
Repeated loud, ere long, by more that come.
Now one can hear that anxious Leaves afar
Are all astir ; and then, 'mid blast and jar,
See Shades, just slumbering, wake on every side,
And round about in strange confusion stride.
And with good cause ! above their swift dismay,
Huge Tempests crowd each peak ; with an array
As terrible, as fallen fiends who went
From black despair to storm the battlement
Of Heaven ! And fiercely, foully do they vie
To break the lines of Light, 'twixt earth and sky!
With sad success ! They carry each redoubt!
And, bounding down with thunder-tread and shout,

Their weapons flash and clash along the rocks,
Where howls the Waste beneath their deathly shocks!

XXIV.

Glancing aside for refuge from the storm,
Lo! I saw men, in diverse dress and form,
Kneeling all round me; and, with less of pride,
I had kneel'd too, had not, just then, my Guide
Said, while he led me toward a shelter near:
"Yes! well may pagan kneel to God! well fear,
When storms like this descend from upper air,
That He, in anger, sits on summits there!
No wonder Greek should deem, in place like this
The home of Superhadean deities!
Here, for his soul conjure those fancied peers,
The scepter'd shadows of foreboding fears!
That Spartan dared not brave Olympus' shocks!
Nor shepherd near Amanus with his flocks!
That Persian bow'd to Bordj, or grand Meru
Subdued the haughty Kooleenu!
Not strange that priests should claim just laws were
 given
On peaks, so far from Earth, so near to Heaven!
Cite, too, palladia, by heathen shown,
And carved with duties, changeless as their stone,
The Thunder's Brontia, Caetylia,
Dread Dysares of hush'd Arabia,
Heliogabalus, Teutonic rainbow urns,
The image which bereaved Pessinus yearns,
Nahadeo, and countless such believed
Warnings, heaven-sent, e'er since The Ten received!
But, think you, 'mid the storms, which is the foe—

Self? or the lightning that lights up its woe?
If sin feel death deserved, no less a due,
If He, who claims a death, the life own too,
Spoke Love or Hate from Sinai's dreaded throne
To give another life, and guard one's own?—
How dear the soul for which men would atone,
What witnesses are sacrifices sad,
From Moloch down to Tauroboliad!"

XXV.

"You yield," I interposed, "much reverence
To heathen worship?" "Yes, there is a sense
In which all faith," said he, "springs from the true.
Denying that, one's choice lies 'twixt the two —
An ignorance to palliate bigotry,
Or else no Christian ground for charity.
And granting that, I deem, who trusts the soul,
Tho' not its fruit sin grafted, trusts the whole,
Trusts God and Revelation, sure to find
But one religion suited for the mind.
Ah, faith there is, whence Doubting seems to be
The haunted fool of flimsiest Misery!—
Of film, whose folds deceptive will transpire,
Whift off by breathing of one live Desire!—
Imagination's freak, appearing wise,
Not when the spirit searches deep to prize
The genuine make of God, but when its reach
Ends with this human-manufactured speech.
Doubt comes to him who courts a wordish war,
And dreams that skill in such is conqueror;
To Surface-Learning, and to fickle Trust,
Dazzled by Creeds that Sight cannot adjust.

Look for the soul! tear sensuous myths! E'en guise,
Deserving well all curse of prophecies,
May show beneath some Truth, not wholly mute,
To teach salvation through a substitute!
Faith! hope! love! longing! deeds by which men rise
From Eden's loss to gain of Paradise!"

XXVI.

We moved to leave the mounts, but soon enslaves
Our Path a blustering Flood. Wide sweep the waves!
They scarce more widely laved lone Ararat,
When erst did cease that voyage long wonder'd at,
While varied tongues and titles spake of one
Noas, Seisithrus, or Deucalion,
Father of men, and farmer of the vine,
With ship and dove their universal sign
To keep that memory of deeds divine!
Long stand we by the waves, and watch their strife.
Then last, he names, as Typhon and his wife,
Dark forms whose cautious footsteps grow along
The mire upon the shore. Soon, muscles strong
By hate, they shove far through the tide a chest
In which the limbs of meek Osiris rest,
The savior of a world they would destroy;
Then sneak away more Virtue to decoy.
Well timed their haste. All Ill is track'd by Good.
Not far, wise Hermes moves to trace the flood,
And name its destined hight. He lifts his brows;

But while he notes their deed, through noiseless
　　boughs
A mellow Light advances toward the stream,
'Mid which, like stars through mists, shine eyes
　　whence gleam
Powers from a soul behind some surface-tears
Unmoved as Heaven beyond Earth's showery fears.
Despite much wrath, despite dishevell'd tress,
Thrice beautiful is Isis in distress!
She hunts for her lost spouse; and with her is
The faithful but abortive Anubis.
Intent upon their aim, they seek great Thoth.
Watch, now, how gods can love whom they be-
　　troth!
How heart can vivify that thing, the face!
Still eyes flash force! substantial muscles trace
The spirit's ebb and flow! emotion pulse
Through moveless cheeks! how very woe exults!
She waves her hand toward Heaven! The gloom
　　withdraws!
Light bursts the sky! and sudden warmness thaws
Thick air that pours adown on tree and sheaf,
And rolls in liquid notes from leaf to leaf;
While, far off from the swift stream's thwarted zest,
Up looms, in free relief, the missing chest!

XXVII.

"Those sacred lips renew the prophecies,"
Explain'd the Guide who mark'd my wondering
　　eyes,
"Of time when Horus shall avenge the death
Of his lost sire who, newly dower'd of breath,

Shall rise in resurrection, rescuing earth
Invoked to share his name and his new birth.
Oft told that prophecy of one, a man
More pure than Noah, saving more of clan
From deadlier floods that Earth dares not to scan;
A fabled hero, from deep shades to spring;
A God incarnate, prophet, priest, or king;
The dream of Art that carved in human scope,
From spotless stone the image of its hope;
What land or age ne'er heard of One to free
From woes of Time and of Eternity?
Not all a man! Man can but pay self's due!
Yet, man in truth, with deeds for manhood, too!"

XXVIII.

"If Heathen hope sought so much that was true,
Tell me," I ask'd, "what profit, then, the Jew?"
"Much, every way," he said, "chief, oversight
Of oracles, amid surrounding night,
Sure types of Truth Reveal'd, and coming Light.
Jews were the chosen few; but, need Control
To bless the chosen, slight the general whole?
Just are the Powers which human Fortunes wield,
Whose accusations then, perchance, are seal'd
Against both Consciousness and Right Reveal'd.
Perchance, those Deeds, which lives depraved re-
    new
Through human means, selected first the Jew
For a peculiar, not a single view
Of truth, truth given for the general cause,
But guarded by one nation's Life and Laws.
And where does candid History that traces

Amid all kinds of castes, and clans, and races,
Find to conserve, a stabler element!
Of all the men against mutation bent,
Spite pasha, pope, king, slaughter, hatred, shame,
But one, the Jew, bides evermore the same.

XXIX.

"Alas! a sect, blest by Omnipotence,
By revelation wise, where ignorance,
Like Esau, bargain'd, through a hungry mind,
Their birthright, to be foremost of mankind,
Exclusive then, as now, possess'd to call, —
As alway pagan priests taught men to call, —
The nation's Guardian, not the Lord of all,
Only of Jew, forgetting prophecy
Which join'd the Gentile name to each decree.
They turn'd from Christ and Him whose power
 above
Has not declared partiality of Love,
Or hope excluded from a part of earth.
The serpent crush'd by heel of human birth,
A Spirit trampling Satan, — with this theme
The whole long records of the prophets teem.
Where is new truth? Where not development
Of sign and sacrifice to all men sent,
Through their first parents? Ah without excuse!
And criminal for adding each abuse,
Stands man himself! Nor human teaching then
Nor now, could ever hide from view I ken —
Despite the gods before Him which men saw
On pictur'd veils vain Fancy hies to draw —
That which the Spirit sways, that higher law

Created with the heart. If circumcised
By faith in Him to whom they sacrificed
Were saved, uncircumcised, tho' dim their pleas,
With faith in Him might equal some of these!

XXX.

"Think you to blame the law of Hebrew priest
That none, save Jonah, was evangelist?
Think you to prove all Words inspired confuse
Which praise God-fearing men who were not Jews?
Paul, truthful ever, need not hint alone
That Greece could worship God, tho' God unknown?
Nor Christ need stoop to use a logic shrewd
To mitigate Samaritanic feud,
Fortelling time when, nay, not here, nor there
The Father should be served, but everywhere?
Oh! could not He, with praises sung in Heaven
By every nation, people, kindred given,
Still keep ideals for all reverent hearts
More chaste than forms which mock'd His nobler parts?
Woe World, if not! all man-pruned history
Grows, for slow shapings to idolatry!
It is not he of heathen name, alone,
Who can bow down to gold and wood and stone!
The ancient priest, to lax tradition given,
For power perverted simple rites of Heaven,
And told of hero, demigod and god:
To-day, with Bible, hidden while they laud,
Which holds the germs, I ween, of all things true,
Lo! not One, mediate 'twixt God and man,

But saint, host, goddess, this Book never knew!
Perchance just Charity would kindlier scan
A Socrates, Athenian gods between,
Who praised a Spirit, for his soul supreme."

XXXI.

Pondering these thoughts, all dead to sight and sound,
I walk'd abstracted, till I mark'd around
Strange, quivering shadows covering the ground.
Yes, the whole air itself seemed thick with shade!
I started then! I peer'd through plain and glade!
On neither side was aught that could be seen;
No mount, nor wood to intercept the sheen!
At last, far, far above, I spied a light,
Higher than clouds could be, the wildest sight
To which I e'er was witness! It came not
From moon or sun; one could not judge from what!
As lightning were if constant, so it glared!
Through each direction tore! and crost! and flared!

XXXII.

Long space the strange scene lasted, till amain
The moon shone from its edge. Far thence, the plain
Upheaved its side to form a giant hill;
And from the top the great ash Yggdrasill,
Beneath one limb of which I now discover
That shaded path had pass'd, is shown to hover
O'er all the north, here resting in the gloom
That broods in west, there animate with bloom,
First blush of Youthful Morn, till thin clouds hide

Dim limbs, like mountain woods, as high as wide!
A sprout 'side this, Aswatha of Hindoo,
Gogard of Persia, Zampuh too
Of Thibet, Kounboun with those mystic signs
That made but little wise its wise divines!
Or tree — whence seeds of these were said to be —
Which tempted Eden to disloyalty.

XXXIII.

We sought its roots: one in the west, where band
The fiends of darkness in their fond Mistland;
And there the serpent lies, like lengthen'd night,
And gnaws the bleeding bark in wallowing spite:
And one, far in the north where Frost-kings dwell,
And, fill'd for wit and wisdom, Mimir's well, —
'Mid its clear depths the mirror'd pole-star fell:
And one, along to east, hard by the morn
And Urdar-fountain, where the patient Norn
Perceives the present, future, and the past,
Nor slights the small, nor shudders at the vast.
Thence, o'er a dread, tempestuous stretch of dark,
The rainbow-bifrost bends, where one can mark
Heimdall the warden his close vigils keep.
Ah! marvelous his ear, e'en in his sleep,
As light as birds, he hears the grasses grow,
And wool on sheep, ten thousand miles below!
Beyond, in grandeur, loom high Asgard homes
Of gods! and there, above those twelve bright thrones,
Gladheim is recognized, with golden domes!
Whence far along Idavollr's placid fields,
Vingolf, secure by hush'd retirement, yields
For Frigga and her kind a wilderness

Of lawns, and lanes, and arbors for recess!
Romantic nights of groves! and days of flowers!
And lakes, and streams, and fairy fountain showers!
A place, where luxury could wish no bliss!
Desire itself be drugg'd to drowsiness!

XXXIV.

But while I gaze upon a scene thus mild,
Storms gather in the heavens, whence clangors wild
Provoke responses fierce! As Lightning flies,
Heimdall on Gulltopp to Valhalla hies,
To find great Odin, and across the plain
More gods pursue, with growing signs of pain!
Here Tyr uplifts, like some vast mountain side,
His ponderous shield that shakes with wounded pride!
There Ullur draws a bow to test his art,
And meteors through remotest heavens dart!
Now Braji leaves Iduna and wise life,
To plan with Forseti a course for strife;
And Frey in haste, through breathless patience wan,
Beats his big boar that saunters slowly on.
Then Freyja with complaining team of gray,
And Vidar, Njord and Vali join the fray;
While through the north, like an Aurora, gleam
The spears of Skadi's troops that nearer stream!
Far up, in Hlidskjalf, towering o'er the crowds,
Like morning Sun enthroned above the clouds,
Bright Odin stands; and, prompt to his command,
Vibrations roll the sea, and rend the land!
Whence comes great Thor whose chariot sweeps the heaven

On flaming wheels of fire to fury driven!
Eclipsing all the rival hosts of light,
As hurricanes trail past the stars of night!

XXXV.

Then, from these ranks conceal'd, I glance below,
To find the threatening cause; wild waste of woe!
The seas, lash'd by the serpent, overflow
All shores! The giant ash, struck by the storm,
Rent and uprooted, reels, a shatter'd form,
And then igniting, like a comet grand,
Burning, with its hot wake, full half the sky,
Plunges far out the limits of the land,
Where soon, in distant dark, the echoes die.
Fire-genii from the deep flame forth with arms
That tear the bifrost down! While this alarms,
Huge giants, 'mid upheaving mounds and cliffs,
Press toward the gods! Soon, where the foul fume
    lifts,
Advance Thor's blazing lines! Of no avail
Is now, alas! their strength! For once, they fail!
For once, can force more dread than their's assault!
And, almost ere they charge, the columns halt!
Then back, through many a lengthening league they
    roll!
Then, wheeling, bend their rivals like a scroll!
Borne back again, for one last charge they form,
As terrible as every earthly storm
Concentrated in one! On! on! they bound!
They blend! oh Soul! my being breaks with sound!
Nor heaven, nor hell could stand so fierce a shock!
But all things!— god or giant! sky or rock!

Or star, or soil! — 'mid bursting fires are hurl'd
Like lava through the air! then all the world
Is smoke, so dense I feel it when I press!
Then all is still! and all is nothingness!

XXXVI.

How long this gloom had place, I cannot tell.
Bewilder'd by the scene and shock, I fell
In shuddering swoon. Waking, my fears dispel.
My Guide is by me; and, tho' hid from sight,
I yet can hear his voice which calms me quite:
"Watch now," says he, "the end of pagan fears,
His good and evil part for endless years."

XXXVII.

Ere long, a slight commotion lures the view.
Amid the shades, gleams here and there flash through
Congealing orbs of gloom, whereat I gaze
With roused attention, and do note that rays
Of light commingle also; and both flow
Apart; the light above; the dark below;
As tho' some chemic power precipitates
All by inherent force to destined fates.
And there, I wis not how, one seem'd to heed
With every moving gleam, or shade, some deed;
And, clinging to each deed, to read a name!
Soon, saw I forms, sometimes with boastful frame,
That look'd, then shrunk below, and sometimes souls
That stood, amazed to find ascending scrolls,

And none descending; till, with mien of praise,
They turn'd, with trembling feet, toward higher ways.

XXXVIII.

At last the long procession had gone by,
And, far beyond me, just against the sky,
I could discover regions, rear'd for Right,
Beyond all beauty beautiful! that sight
No man could see, and deem one other bright!
All glare of earth, in one lens, were a blot
Beside those shining pinnacles! nay! not
In all the tales, by seer or sibyl given,
One thing suggested like that scene in Heaven.
And then, how could I, from a view so dear,
Look down? I could not. Such a Heaven near,
Hades or Helheim could but prompt to fear.
And "one," thought I, "grows much less pure in
 Time,
From fear of ill than hope of the sublime."

XXXIX.

But yet, I doubted, till, half turn'd toward place
Where souls, descending, went, lo! I did face
A mighty Light that brighten'd earth and sky,
So bright, I thought, because this Light was nigh,
All things that I had pass'd appear'd so clear
In the dim night; and, gazing forward here,
It seem'd to light the way far as that heaven.
'Twas on a little knoll, the splendor given
From rays that fell and glanced, stronger before,
Weaker behind, from off a cross! "But more,"
My Guide said, "waits us, while we have this Light
'Tis our work to advance from sight to sight."

XL.

Soon valleys deep and dark did hide the scene,
Where all was gloom, save here and there some
    sheen
From warring weapons. Then came place of dread:
'Mid reeking shades, unnumber'd heroes dead!
Myriads of captives, into bondage led!
And gladiatorial thousands, kill'd to grace
The civilization of its populace!
Anon, however, when the haze unrolls,
Far more distinct, loom individuals.
"Look!" says my Guide: "Men find their king a
    man!
And he finds other claims than self's to scan!
Those restless fetters of the slave flash fire!
And they are loosed that all wish may aspire!
Lo! churches, homes, and missions far extend!
And seas, where crowding ships of commerce wend,
Sails set to work with winds from heaven above,
And mingle language, custom, art and love!
But watch men here:" which done, I understood
How few remark'd the universal good,
In search of things minute, and hard to glean,
Whence scowls of discontent scrimpt many a mien
That peer'd through lens, with all the light he had
In hope, I learn'd, to magnify the bad!

XLI.

Among the throng was one who came to us.
"These Times," said he, "these Times degener-
    ous

Bid one yield up to new Desires that lurch
The blood-stain'd standards of One Holy Church.
The Church is home of all that Love has taught,
Or deed has gain'd, or Laws humane have sought,
'Mid troubled floods, the only ark of heaven:
Blest are those halls where parent vows are given,
Where young susceptive lips are train'd to pray,
Where life grows constant to the holy way,
Blest are those simple rites, the quiet throng,
The thrilling organ, and the mutual song,
The prayers and pleadings, thoughts, decisions wise,
The still walk home, the present Paradise!
Cursed the soul whose mad conceit would sate,
Lessening the sovereignty of its estate.
For twenty centuries this power has kept
The older creeds for faith that fear'd and wept,
And outlived Heathendom and Heresy" —
"Yes," said my Guide, "and that Truth might be
 free,
Made free its forms! Cursed is age or youth
That clings to such, when such can fetter Truth!"

XLII.

"Alas!" the first rejoin'd, "with truth your search
You find no good, no profit in the Church?"
"Much every way!" was answer'd, "chiefly, aye,
Just as the Jew was once, the Church to-day,
Great in the Truth reveal'd! What plea the Jew
To slight those forms ordain'd by prophets true
One hour before the greater Lamb reveal'd
The law of sacrifice in type repeal'd?
What plea the Church to slight one Bible-fact

That furthers faith in heart or good in act?
Or how, while mental errors can pollute
A soul's ideals of the Absolute,
Can young or old slight conference, and not stray
Far from the right? Well that for all a sway, —
Though temple, altar, priesthood pass'd away, —
The people's synagogue remain'd, to be
The same power as of yore, with ministry
Preserving 'mid the best life visible
The truth once given, which no man can annul,
Or change, or mystify! that this remain
Till some new dispensation shall make plain
To soul of every individual
Truth partial now, and perfect but in all.
Ah! in old time, — and, if no single man
Have love or truth complete, wisely, I scan, —
Faith sought its Sovereign's voice through Charity
That asks report from each! and so, may be,
In matter of mere form, Faith should again,
Like James, Paul, Peter, and those brethren,
Waive word and whim to further deed and choice. —
They serve the Church, who serve the Spirit's
    voice."

XLIII.

"Ah!" sigh'd the stranger, then, right mournfully,
"So many claim it, where can this voice be?"
"Nations, there are," my Guide said, "one alone
Through kindred traits, and one upon the throne,
By generous laws, most strong in central life,
Spite of provincial tax, and local strife. —
You deem the Church divided? Who are you,

So sure how Christ can best preserve in view
Himself the Sovereign still of all things true?
Voice is, whence Faith may serve a Godless shrine,
And worship human things, and not divine;
Not Truth reveal'd in Bible or in heart,
But human systems added to a part,
Priestly tradition, fact mixt up with lies,
Interpretation, wordish compromise,
Thought of the Spirit struggling out to view
Too wide-aberrant from direction true
Through fleshy medium! Patience, Heart, a truce!
Here are but earthen vessels, with best use
Too frail and scant to bear without abuse
All that the soul holds! If Church Government
Need forms for self, like a wise man content
To rule through ruling self, so let it sway.
It has not standards absolute, for fray
'Gainst duteous love for Him of peaceful way,
Because corps-colors differ! Loyal Hearts
May guard, and may advance through better arts
Their Church, the Church of truth. Naught, I aver,
Thrives less through force than truthful character.

XLIV.

"And naught can rear more reverent Piety
Than Thought content to wait till it can see,
Profaning not through explanations given
Those deeper symbols, clear alone to Heaven.
Systems there are, so part and join control,
That who profess, profess to know the whole.
There is not left one notch for mystery;
And, without mystery, no faith can be;

Nor without faith, religion. Ah! I trow,
The moods most loving claim far less to know;
Remembering men walk by faith, not sight,
And, therefore, charity alone is right:
Or if they plead, remembering they who speak
Through angel tongues, without this are but weak.
Have you forgotten, 'twas a bigot claim
Made pharisee and pope both lose their aim;
Kill'd Christ; and, if it dared, might kill him now
Who, with the self-same spirit, bid one bow
Not, for the public eye, to priest or art,
But to the God who gazes on the heart?
Truth! Truth is Sovereign, not the speech! nor sect!
Who love God's Truth love God! Yes! I detect,
Who most search this, kneel most to mystery!
First, faithful here, and then to what shall be!
If Heaven fail them — it sooner fails the worm,
Faithless to Him who sends the Reason storm,
Skulking from Light beneath an earthly form!"

XLV.

"I fear such slight of form," the first replied.
"Lax laws but cause lax life." "Ah," said my Guide;
"If Church, like Nation struggling to be wise,
Relax restriction that true Worth may rise,
And leave Desire all form Desire should prize,
Or royal or republicanic, still
It is not Anarchy best sways the Will!
Nay! nay! The flimsiest charity on earth,
Thinner than bigot's! — he would aim at worth —

Has mood that dare profane in plan or mirth
The Power, by which souls, taught of God, are brought
To reverence Right, ere strong to handle thought.
If there be place where virtue is sustain'd;
Where youth and ignorance seem safely train'd;
There meek Responsibility must tread,
Conforming where, through forms, the Right is led!
Thence Charity — Life's final victory,
Because Health cannot love all equally —
Yields not the free lust of the prostitute, .
But Love's expression, where Command is mute;
Where Bible vague, there it, lest Impious Strife
Tear at the veil which God has hung to life!
Loyal to well tried form, this Grace, I see,
At home, ward Thought too crude for liberty,
Abroad, beneath much talk of diverse creed,
Searching the heart, the source of all pure deed,
Hoping that there, tho' words and ways may vie,
Is possibility of unity;
That there, where is the real throne of Life,
Dwells Wish to influence without a strife,
Desire for truth whence Love may win consent
As mild as He who in the garden bent,
Nor needed sword, nor more expedient.
Elsewise, behold fact for yourselves:" he said.
Then gazed we from a place to which he led.

XLVI.

There was descried a brightest realm in view;
And many thronging thither, tho' but few

In haste did seem to reach it. On the way
They would pause much, with much to scan, and
    say
Of things about. Still they would move apace;
And whither moved, I mark'd a spacious place,
Yet crampt by buildings; here by chapels small,
There by cathedrals; and, when nigh them, all
Did diverse homage, cross self, or bow down,
With holy glance at dress of black or brown;
Or, still erect, clasp hands of friends, or some,
With folded hands, wait but for love to come.

XLVII.

We, too, drew nigh; soon forced, like most, I
    ween, —
Though one could trace, too, those of humbler
    mien, —
To watch the throngs most zealous to be seen.
Ere long, was heard loud talk, where men admired,
What God — so fear'd the soul — had not inspired.
Past that, a fretful Zest coaxt peaceful boon
From pitying Spirits sought through sigh and
    swoon.
Further, 'mid crowds with cover'd heads or bare,
Broad-brimm'd or narrow-brimm'd of hat or hair,
Sped weary gasping sounds, found out as prayer
From Providential print men bent to there.
Then music lured. We had join'd with some choir,
For praise was rife, but none did lead desire;
Only soft throats seem'd thankful for much hire;
Or fearing art, too chill by doggerel,
Tones shut from draft of blowing organ's swell;

Or fearing Nature, chords in place made drear
That candles, or a smoky atmosphere,
Or worth of well-stain'd glass make Heaven ooze
 near.
Search tired. Still thought I, "Not alone for me,
True Spirit Life has forms, like nature, free
To grow from One Power, yet Infinitely!"

XLVIII.

Just then, one sauntering by, cried, "Mark you
 there!
New priests! like nurses, faithless to their care,
Who, feeding sweets to Sense and Selfishness,
Do coax wrong Passion on to Life's distress,
These soothe the soul when thoughts of sin perplex,
Not by pure thoughts of God, lest conflict vex,
But by dumbfounding tones of men and boys,
By bows and beads, sole trace of household joys,
With hints that faith may live in ears and eyes,
To damn the ignorant and distract the wise!"

XLIX.

"Let Facts speak!" said my Guide; while, 'mid
 the scene,
Disputes did rise. Alas! for Life serene!
Logic left Truth reveal'd, talk'd cant, and creeds,
Worship devoid of love, and faith of deeds.
Soon, humblest souls, I saw, who had come there
In search of faith; they shunn'd each place of
 prayer
In still distaste, or doubt, or wild despair.
Near by gloom'd an abyss! In swift retreat

Full many crowded that way! thence their feet
Slipt, amid cries too late to save from loss!—
And down they fell where no light and no cross!

L.

"Ah!" sigh'd my Guide, "what wisdom does not know
That Earth, not Heaven, has made religion so?
With life a mystery of mysteries,
What comfort has the soul that thoughtful is,
Save trust in God? that source of life, unseen?
Life may join all things. Suns, with stilly mien,
Draw to thin clouds thick water from the mire,
To cause the thunder of the lightning's fire!
Troubles bring doubt! and doubt philosophy!
And even Love finds schools in bigotry!
Why not in sects, if shape to benefit,
Be less the truth itself, than made for it?
Once Tyrant Form taught Faith of liberty:—
What shall the Present teach? Oh, Hope! set free
That Charity which ·cannot prompt us long,
Ere all must join in one prayer, and one song!

LI.

" E'en now Truth comes to many a separate search.
Who doubts that publican, whate'er his Church,
May breathe through some dead body of a prayer
A Spirit's sigh to fetch the answer there?
Who can deny to ways that freest roam
The yearnings of a more methodic home?
Ah! they who trust alone to Sovereign might,
Find out there's much to do, to do the right!

And they who boast the power of human will,
Oft fail, to feel their need of Mercy still!

LII.

"I deem, through ways diverse, like mighty wings
Of some vast army, Truth, advancing, brings
First one, and then the other toward the foe,
With mingling stratagem, not best to show,
Fickle to sight, mysterious to maintain
The progress, slow but sure, of central gain.
'Mid Theory to trust, in wise defense,
Faith, tho' it mourn, may watch with confidence
These partial victories of Partial Right.
We learn! — tho' all the Forms that loom in sight
Be controverting Facts, for ever nigh,
Just past this range of human Theory!

LIII.

"With all religious life from oldest sign
Deeds which have sprung from faith in deeds divine,
Better not doubt the soul's truth, trust it rather.
Tho' deist tell but fact of God the Father,
Humanitarian speak alone of Son,
Or pantheist of Spirit, truth is one!
And tho' the lips may limit and confine,
Speech is a human thing; the soul divine!
For it remains a Heaven, where Faith can rest,
Tho' Thought seek systems better than the best;
Whence all that is not true shall cease to be;
Whence all that is have power for unity:
Till found, we wait; till some Columbus here
Shall sail about this other, grander sphere,
And prove at last how ways, while parting, near!

LIV.

"Who shall he be to test for skeptic minds
This gravitating law of love which binds?
Thought, Thought, that long since systematized the star,
'Tis time it moved to find out what we are!
'Tis time this wandering World's Philosophy
Return to its first love of Unity!
Not like the Greek, to water, air, or fire,
But mindful ever of the life!—desire!
With proof to spring and end in argument,
From consciousness, for conscience reverent,
Its premises, like touch in sympathy!
Its logic, like to life in certainty!
Hope must it speak for age! and faith for youth!
A substance, with expression only truth!
For substance, with existence only love!
Oh if such thrive not here, it shall above,
Where He, who most regards the Spirit's weal,
Bids Faith prevail, when Learning learns to kneel."

LV.

He paused: then said—"Each reverential Star
Draws back where nears the Sun. My home is far:
Now, that our feet approach, once more, the dell
Where first we met, I must away: farewell!"
"Farewell!" both said; and, turning, he had gone.
But I awaited still the coming dawn.
And, pondering much the scenes we had pass'd by,
Resolved, ere high the sun or broad the sky,
They should not lack a tale to testify.

SOL.

LIMBS of the dying body ache with toil,
   But the undying mind when most unused:
Nature abhors a vacuum, no less
Than her true children all things void in life.
These need not wait like thoughts to implant the like,
But from much wish oft germinate what lacks,
And bear most fruit where grown 'mid most of dearth:
Had some such dearth inspired these thoughts on Love? —
Their scribe was one, now long a bachelor,
Proud most of proud indifference, seen ne'er
To turn and watch God's beauty in a face,
Or bend his eyelids to a neighboring tear
Where Pain pass'd by in wailing agony,
Or e'en lose rein of smiles, tho' nature 'd shaken
All jostling incongruities in one: —
So said the village gossip. — Ah, but Earth,
Serves he the least or most who guardeth best
The holy shrine of an Ideal Life,
Nor draws the veil to one impertinence? —
None solved this problem in the bachelor.
But long it was before the electric smile
That chased the glancing fire about the room,
What time the title came, had played away.

POEM FIFTH.

LOVING.

I.

LIFE is a mystery, mystery bound;
   Above, about, unrest profound;
Behind, a dream of the soul's dim home;
Before, a scheme for the mist and the foam.
The winds drive on: we shudder, but steer:
We tack for comfort; but drift in fear:
We cry for help; but struggle alone;
Or gain no gain, that is all our own.
We pray for Heaven: if Heaven be near,
Some beacons of peace are glimmering here.
Philosophy come, search far! search wide!
Past Passion and Prejudice, Precept and Pride.
With Heaven the haven, life cannot dispense
With a sigh of the spirit, or sight of the sense.

II.

Where, where is good? The world has claims:
If claiming from each, then each has aims:
And all the wide world is too vast for the plan
That looms to the scope of any one man:
WE MUST DIVIDE!
FOR THE WAYS ARE WIDE!

III.

This hear I commanded,
  Through shadows withdrawn,
'Mid light that expanded
  Creation's first dawn!
Off fly to their missions
  The systems and stars
To stores of fruitions
  Infinity bars:
And high heave the mountains:
  And broad stretch the plains:
And up burst the fountains:
  And down fall the rains:
And fragrant
  And beautiful,
    Herbage and flower:
And vagrant
  And dutiful
    Manhood, a power!
    Our glory
    It is
    Time's story
    Is this.
  The spirit of life
  Is a spirit of strife.
The calmest and best of us is but a knight
Whose rest is the weariness won in the fight:
  And the purpose of deed is the promise of life.
The world whirls away: we spring to our gage:
And bustle and jostle from childhood to age!

IV.

  Lo! the feeble wails
   Of an infant voice,
  Too young for the tales
   Of a wandering choice!
The weary eyes shrink from the points of the stars,
 From touch of the glance of the world that is.
The ears are shaken by treads and jars!
 The face looks fright to mysteries!
The small hands clutch for motes of the air;
 For plaits of the dress; for folds of the bed;
But marvels move, and mingle, and tear,
 Redoubled by every shred!
The feet that balance the tottering brain
Steal out the sly door; and soak in soft rain;
Or stumble, with shrieks, for barbarian joys,
The roar and the rush of terrible boys!
And wheels that grind omnipotent noise!
Or call: "My mother! the flowers are sweet!
My mother! look out! see the long, long street!
And all the big houses! Oh! what do they do,
Those strange, strange people that don't know
  you?—
That fat, funny thing! it kicks and it cries!—
 How can we be like one another?
Why don't it come here from the naughty flies,
 Come here then, and have a dear mother?"

V.

The lone, little being, all wilder'd by needs,
And thoughts that it can't speak, or nobody heeds,

Oh, where can it find any respite or rest,
But there, again, on that cherishing breast,
Its hope, — the comfort, so many times given,
Its faith, — that of saints in God and in Heaven!

VI.

Yes, Heaven! it too for the soul has aims!
If claiming from each, to each it proclaims:
    For love, one end
    Where all things blend:
        WE MAY UNITE!
        FOR THE WAYS ARE BRIGHT!

VII.

And lo! when words have been spoken,
    The words of no other,
The little life that had broken
    Is join'd to the mother!

VIII.

Rest there, gentle Infant! in all of thy years
The world cannot furnish for haven from tears
    A calmer or constanter love.
Take heart thence for service if parent be wise
To yield to young longings, if Charity prize
    Weak nature as moulded above.

But, ah! if the unwise welcome thy fears
With spirit directing toward storms of the years,
    More bent to their wish than thy good,
The first of all parents could no more undo
Than those of the present whose self-seeking, too,
    Gives birth both to nature and mood!

God guide the home-handling! The frail is no
    fiend :
Where powers still latent lurk, waiting till wean'd.
    God speed but the weaning of Love!
Love bide, howe'er guided! The Will is no wreck
With truth to confide, and age to protect,
    So wish may be aided above.

IX.

Oh Maidenhood! learn to be mothers!
    Lest the babe move away
While the training it gains not from others
    Your doubtings delay.
Instinctive to spiritual birth,
    And impulse of growth,
'Twill leap from you o'er the earth,
    No matter how loath,
To mingle its feeble means in the strife,
Where the stoutest of us must battle for life.

What culture we need in the mothers!
    Of wisdom what wealth!
Those slender limbs mould as few others
    To outlines of health.
And when the little eye dims
    To its trifles of quest,
All quaint of its wonders and whims,
    She, she must give rest.
And the petty desire of that tenderer tone
To God is as great and as dear as her own.

What work to be done by the mothers!
    What stimulant given! —

A love, to grow broad as all brothers,
 And high as the Heaven;
The precepts of living explain'd
 From cradle to school;
And thought to be planted and train'd
 For the sage or the fool;
All the woe that our Earth could inherit from Eve,
Through woman again to lessen and leave.

X.

But swiftly, too swiftly hies time:
 Mark! immature moods, grown strong,
Outgrow all the nursery rhyme,
So potent in earlier prime,
 Hush'd sadly, to feel, ere long,
WE MUST DIVIDE!
FOR THE WAYS ARE WIDE!

XI.

The school-house bell!
What a tale does it tell
To the child who, first, with book and slate
And bounding step for the pictured fate,
Goes out from home where the dear eyes yearn,
Out into the world, with a world to learn!
 Alas! for the soul that sought for change!
 Those crowds before
 Fall back from the door,
With a chill, wide space for the strange;
Until, to the gaze of quizzical boys,
 His hopeful face

Drops, shy apace ;
  For he walks alone ;
  And has hush'd the tone   .
Of all that was fond in joys.
Ah then to his vision the earth grows dim,
More cheery without, more sad with him !
And the pride that shuns disparaging looks
Unweariedly wrestles for worth in books.

XII.

  The school and its sport !
  What a world they import
To the youth, when both appear old !
When shrinking nerves become bold !
And, toughen'd past tilts, once seeming so stout,
Self wheels, in turn, to test all about !
  Alas ! for the master that hoped him wise !
    The questions are miss'd
    At the head of the list,
  And a younger carries the prize.
  But, if, from a hight of love and of zeal,
    The teacher inspire
    Through toils that tire,
    What nobler throne
    Can Honor own ?
  What station, surer of weal ?
There is life that moves with a brighter train :
There is power for winning more glitter of gain :
Retired but God-like, naught more dear
To others and self than the mission here.

XIII.

  The school, with its cares!
  What a life there prepares
For the man of right or of wrong!
For the great, perchance, then least of the throng,
Whose compass, through all those whims of his,
Was a conscience, stronger than mysteries!
  The first in the start may fail of the race;
    For far is the crown
    Where rank is renown,
  And many allure to the base.
  The hand that steadies the rudder from ill,
    And minds but duty
    And waits for booty,
    Steers clear of offense,
    To grow conqueror thence:
  The test of life's pilot is will.
For the course of earth is a course of toil;
The sooner we learn it, the less we recoil:
Who rounds at the goal of the world with joy,
Learn'd this in the little world, when a boy.

XIV.

  The new has claims
    That the old has not:
    How much for games
    Is the home forgot!
There is sport for green, and river, and hall;
Kite and see-saw, fishing and ball;
Clubs for rhetoric, reading, and fun;
Books to study and slight and shun:

And fresh little thoughts spring, clinging to each,
With a wonderful blooming of high-color'd speech;
And, quick and sensitive, bare of all sheath,
A marvelous action of life beneath,
More honest and valiant for half of the right
Than your older ways, with little more light;
With feeling! with feeling! Ah! that is the thing!
And over the world the Spirit will sing,
UNITE! UNITE!
FOR THE WAYS ARE BRIGHT

XV.

The child-life dodges the stare
   And test of spectacled age.
It sighs for something to spare
   The microscope of the sage.
Sad, after the prize has been won;
   Sad, after the cheer of the throng;
Sad, after the parent's "well done;"
   Oh what is the thing that is wrong?
He knows not till, flushing of face,
   With eyes that the heart shines through,
Forsaking the shout and the chase,
   One follows his steps that withdrew.
He knows not till feelings and aims,
   As timid, yet tired of control,
Throw off all the form that restrains,
   And touch their soul to his soul.
Oh joy of the Spirits in Heaven!
   Is it this? — No checking of shame,
Naught, naught to be hid or forgiven,

Constraining communion of aim?
And can all the twist of the creeds
  Entangle true faith in the days
When nothing of selfishness pleads,
  And naught of utility sways? —
For the world and its ways have been given
  To speak to the sense of the soul;
And naught in the Bible or Heaven,
  But love feels a part of the whole!

XVI.

Romance is a dream
  That age must esteem;
For none whom it never possest,
Were ever the bravest or best!
The soul, moved most by the earth,
  Is sensitive first to a part.
'Tis virtue would open to worth;
  'Tis vice seeks earlier art.
A pledge of honor begun,
  Temptations will fail
While deeds of the confident shun
  What caution must veil.

XVII.

Yes! Love is a sovereign, far too rare
For Pelf to touch, or a Lie to dare!
A hallow'd sovereign where awed Delight
Must ever worship in robes of white,
For ever reverent, kneel to see
The shrine of its homage in mystery!
True Love has a life for the inmost heart,

Content in closeted hours to impart
Its whisper'd praises! amid the throng,
Tho' tones more mellow fill word and song,
      Enough in feeling,
      Without revealing,
      One eye in walking,
      One ear in talking,
One heart exultant at well earn'd pride: —
To tattle of love were suicide!
Self sates in that service of sweetest pain,
  Oppressing with too much worthiness;
In airy beauty, ideal of reign,
  Who'd dare to breathe on a bubble of bliss!
      One ruder grasp,
      It dodges the clasp.
The veil of that Holy of Holies is torn
By moods meant not, when temper is worn.
      The glory has flown
      One impious tone.
      The boy is right
      Who weeps in the night.

XVIII.

  Dear vows, they are meant when made,
Of Friendship, forever to last.
  But, where the gleam laid
  Can the sun send shade,
When the bright, high noon is past.
  But, even the night
  Has a holy light;
And, whenever the day return again,
  There's a spot that the same

Old sun will inflame;
For the soul there are joys, tho' the boys have grown men.

XIX.

How soon the tints of morn are away!
Come sounds of storm! come skies, so gray!
    To the sense above
    All may seem love:
Our lower minds, to the right jejune,
When the calls for work begin to tune,
May hear not chords that the whole is giving,
But only a part, and misjudge living.
Whatever the truth, life must decide
Not, not from the World that aye replied:
DIVIDE! DIVIDE!
FOR THE WAYS ARE WIDE!

XX.

There comes a time, none can postpone,
When all must move into life alone;
Must choose for right; or choose for wrong;
And the path they take is a path life-long.
What tho' some milder memories know
Nor hour, nor year, that turn'd them so?
What tho' some shrink from the woes before
With a shock that is never forgotten more?
All eyes had watch'd those paths of change,
Till naught that came seem'd wholly strange:
And tho' but little of virtue or vice
    In thought of earth or of skies,
These whims to wishes and ways entice;
    And steps must follow the eyes.

Ah, so I know,
With mercy for all,
No matter how small
The thought of things to endure,
Our first cure of sin
Is not to begin,
And to keep the memory pure.

XXI.

There are many paths where good can guide:
Whichever they take, men must divide.
And not one slight of the world is forgot:
Some snob will snuffle at every lot.
 Clear bent for the best is quoted as bad:
Once John had a devil: once Christ was a sot:
  Our toil — what of it? — is lonely and sad.
But God made all, despite the throng
Who rank His difference right and wrong.
God rules: then, perchance, we are wiser for act
Which learns from feeling as much as from fact,
E'en taught, through the injuring zeal of our race,
That gentleness too is a Christian grace;
E'en taught with Him whose patience mild
Spake once — to point the man to the child.

XXII.

How much we need that lesson, alas!
We sally forth: we mix with the mass:
We meet the world: and it scoffs, to show
How little about the world we know.
  When only a boy,
  To know a little, that was our joy:

But, now, to the man
Temptations begin as Adam's began.
Like him we all would be gods; and boast
All knowledge from under to uppermost.
The day we mourn a limit of call,
We choose the means to conquer or fall;
By faith in the Infinite Spirit above
To master ourself, to accept with love
A partial dower,
And that concentrate into a power;
Or choose the means, where a wide Pretence
That weakens the fortress of sure defence
Shall yield to attack when the first surprise
With the boasted front of the hypocrite vies.
Earth! Earth! win you that trial of woe,
How suddenly old these young hearts grow! —
They cease to mature in truth, too proud
To ask one boon of the vaunting crowd.
They cease to mature in love that lends
No more than frailty borrows of friends.
They cease to mature in Godship, and trust
The rank of the world that ranks by lust.
Earth! Earth away! nor tempt to that mould!
There's a brand for death from the stamp you hold:
And but one life of perpetual youth,
And that from faith in the Spirit of Truth.

XXIII.

Ye too, vain souls! with some truth to praise,
When will ye learn
How much ye earn

For wrong and the world by bigoted ways?
  Tho' spirit of party may win
  By rating its opposite, "sin,"
    To ponder and halt
    Is seldom all fault;
    A natural smile,
    It never is guile;
But many a false array of Zeal
Has frighten'd the honest Truth from weal:
And many a blast of pious hate
Is blown by the devil to rouse his mate.
  Oh how dare a Christian libel —
    What widen with light
    But never are trite —
  The right and wrong of the Bible?
Enlarge and lessen, as self inspires
The fretful fancy of peevish desires? —
So guilt and innocence blend in the end:
Such serve but what they are willing to lend.

XXIV.

Let Spirit of Charity sway,
With patience for virtue that vice may away!
  Ye zealots, believe!
The rude can only train to deceive;
And the stench of a marsh, that breath of a lie,
Before or behind there's a vice that is nigh.
Praise God for all frankness! To zest of the boy
Leave innocent whim, tho' but vapory joy,
But the mount cascade of the earlier stream,
Too soon, too soon comes end of the dream:

   Away, away
    Float spatter and spray;
But, surely as rills roll on to the sea,
The pure depths flow to Eternity!
Life's Love, that royal life of the soul,
Who'll kill?—No greater exists to control:
But Patience, its offspring and equal, may out:
To love, this is wisdom need wait for no doubt!

XXV.

The thought is of action, but ardor to till,
   Or weaker or stronger,
   Is not supreme longer,
When real life matches ideals of will.
For life is love's center, a myth without this,
And, sooner or later, we know of the bliss:
The goblet of Time, it fills to the brim:
Live high! is the cry, till the dizzy eyes swim!
Live high! and the glass, it jingles and clashes!
We drink, till we reel, the hot fire as it flashes!
The world, it whirls around and around—
Oh soul, is the center of being, then, found?
So bright, ne'er the world! they are stars that sur-
  round;
'Tis Heaven! high Heaven! hark! hark! the
  spheres sound:
     Unite! Unite!
     For the ways are bright!

XXVI.

Oh Search that was longest, Oh World that was wide,
Oh Heart that was toss'd on a compassless tide,

Waves, wild of commotion, ye hush into rest,
For there, beyond, looms the land of the blest!

Oh Eyes that had strain'd for the form of delight,
Oh Ears that had listen'd the long, long night,
Oh Hands that claspt vaguely what dropt from, you
    dead,
By guile of the phantom no more be misled.

'Tis Truth that here welcomes. Oh Beauty, thy
    beams
Have burn'd through all mists that obscured thee in
    dreams!
Ne'er blush of a cheek so bloom'd to confess;
Ne'er Purity spotless, so pledged in the dress.

Come hither and conquer, oh Spirit of Love!
Oh Captive-Heart flutter! thy life hies above!—
Sweet death, to be dying from pierce of an eye!
To fall, and be lifted to live in the sky!

On, dearest of Seraphs! they lie who would trace
Aught dearer in holier, happier race.
The reverent spirit yields to the sight—
It yieldeth to God where love is the might.

XXVII.

In the day transfiguring earth and skies,
    How blest is the light of a confidence sure
    What Power makes all life be and endure!
It comes when, filling with love, we rise
    Regenerate by the Spirit of Truth:
It comes with assent that glorifies
    A soul possessing Ideal of youth.

Ne'er sang the birds so thrillingly sweet!
And ne'er so clear the rills at the feet!
   The leaves are all flowers!
   And crystal all showers!
Through the clouds come green hills, growingly
   grand,
Like the nearing shores of a Spirit-land!
And those red stars burn into the soul!
We melt far out in a calm control!
We faint in the lap of the fragrant air!
So dear! so dear! we die to all care.
Ay, she that has won in that moment of bliss,
Holds all Immortality worth not this!
Nay, nay, we have gain'd the life above —
Who'd dare to deny it to our first love? —
We have, we have Eternity!
But bright suns rise, to set, may be.
How blest are they who never find out
How earthly love, like its home, shifts about!

XXVIII.

What is Hell? Ah mark it! there's life on earth
Bleedingly torn from all it is worth:
Things are rent that nature allied:
Wish and all of its ways divide.
Hope there is, wretchedness! love there is, death!
Bodies for feeling, yet feeling all breath!
Faith that is fickle! and freak that stays!
Scorchings forever! yet chills from the blaze!
Music, yet misery! cheering, yet groan!
Cherish'd one hated! and crowded, yet lone!
White wings, clipt, that spatter in mud!
Stars to look at, and dirt for a cud!

XXIX.

What wisdom is this, the elders presage,
That frankness of feeling must wait upon age?
Perhaps it were better, in life's growing prime,
To live to our nature than cater for crime.
Love, rarest of passions, with burnings untold,
It melteth the being, to turn out the gold:
One sound of its kindling, vice hears as a knell,
And sinks from that Heaven, as far as to Hell.
Perhaps it were manlier, nobler, for most
To live, while they live, than delay for the ghost:
While all that is in them is yearning to band,
Give heart for acceptance, as well as a hand.
Accursed, all civilized, cautious alloy
That weakens true virtue, or lessens true joy,
That dams into calmness the flow of the heart,
To winter the icy sparkle of art.

XXX.

One seeks not to rhyme
An excuse for a crime
Who speaks but a truth that is true in all time,
And says that the art
Of breaking the heart
Is not confined to one sex, in the start.

Who are they that dance
With early romance,
And beacon all Nature to love, with a glance?
They are girls who decoy
The more modest boy
To truth but a flash, for faith but a toy.

  Who are they that start
  Their hand for the heart,
Then fling down the mitten, to see how we smart?
  They are maids who propose
  We love as do those
Who have flirted their limited lot to a close.

  Who are they enjoin
  The beauty of coin,
And shrug, if we doubt of the soul they purloin?
  They are matrons who trade
  The life of the maid,
And mention a match as a bargain, well paid.

  Who are they that sigh
  As we question the why:
"There's nothing like learning, you'll learn· by
  and by"?
  They are women who teach
  Young honor a speech,
To ruin all others that come in its reach.

XXXI.

Oh ′soul that found living so sacredly sweet,
Can things that we worship collapse into cheat?
High Spirit of Faithfulness, what! hast thou died?
Can Love kneel prostrate, and yet be denied?
Fond Promise that lured to the marvels above,
Nor hinted that Hatred was tracking on Love,
Can manhood be led up so far, but to fall?
And must farewell be the end of it all?

Go Memory, vanish! Come Reason to Rage.
There's nothing that smarts, but health may assuage.
Away with a madness that hasted to be:
What Ridicule follows let Influence flee!
To push and to paddle the rill of a rhyme,
Scant waters beneath, and a scanty sublime, —
Out, out of such folly! here now to the land!
Farewell! Oh Wisdom! give vigor to stand!

Farewell — ah, to feel it! — farewell to the dream!
There's something far better in life, than to seem;
Far better, with glory to win or to miss,
Than languidly lulling the doll of a bliss!
Let love unrequited live not, to control:
'Tis the fancy of feeling, the foam of the soul! —
Yet Life, how much dearer! could reason and right
Still prosper with pleasure! Farewell to the light! —

Farewell to delusion! Let truth but appeal!
Hark, rises a din! See, flashes a steel! —
What bodes in the distance? — Now gird on with might! —
It may be to conquer! — it must be to fight! —
Mount! — In with the spurs! — The trumpet! — Away!
The crowning of bliss come after the fray! —
Charge up! and charge onward! — The field, it is wide —

Farewell to the phantom! — Here's life! — It had
    lied!
DIVIDE! DIVIDE!
FOR THE WAYS ARE WIDE!

XXXII.

Oh why do we sever, despoiling the heart?
With groans for pleasure, and cheers for smart,
We buckle in feeling; we buckle on pain:
We tighten the nerves, that tingle and sprain:
We wrench at the heart's frail strings, until
We've snapt the tenderest cords, with our skill:
And Life's sweet music? there's no more tune!
We dig in the earth, down, down for a boon,
Where never comes sun; where never comes moon
Nay! that's not half of the woe, not half!
We lie to our nature: we twit, and we laugh:
    We dare
        To jeer of the friendship gone:
    We dare, yet there
        Are Christ and John.

XXXIII.

There are times when the meanest man bows down
To hide in the dirt his dress of the clown.
But the meanest man, he bows too late:
His eyes are red, and his lips inflate.
Don't buy, tho' cheap, that ruffian:
The sweet is the seasoning not the man.
Whatever the maids have left in the bowl
Is handled and hack'd to the hash of a soul.

As well trust apples of Sodom! — with gnashes,
Who tastes that dainty bites in the ashes.
As well pursue a Will-o'-Wisp's flare! —
That fire of devotion is all in the air.
As well touch a carcass! — those pulsings avow'd
Are worms that are crawling round under a shroud.
No beauty of soul is there; gross is the beast:
The source, not the right, of repentance has ceast.
The Spirit Ideal, that would woo above,
Drive off! and have hell! where nothing to love!

XXXIV.

Some more, some less, with little to love,
All, all of us leave the sky to the dove.
We delve away, in the depth of our trade;
And all are dusty before well paid.
Some like the dust; some mourn its need;
And some gaze cheerly toward end of the deed.
The most sink, prostitutes hugging to all,
Good bad or indifferent, beauty or scall,
 Till each love Christ would have kept
 Dies out of the man, unwept;
Love's natural hate of the deeds unkind,
 It pleads from the face no blush:
 There bides but the counterfeit flush,
The paint that allures to the lust left behind.

XXXV.

 What power can save
 When Forms would enslave?
Shall one, when the foes' ranks wide enroll,
  Forget his soul?

With every flag of a high cause furl'd,
Yield up the fight?—a man of the world
Who struggled once, was conquer'd thence,
And squats like a beggar that smirks for pence,
  Who dandles his palms
  And storms and calms,
For a paltry pittance or pride to please
With a sneer for those, and a smile for these?

XXXVI.

Nay, nay, oh Faith! Good giveth a goal
Where will itself wills life for the soul.
Him, buried below, breath blesses above,
And duty on earth aye journeys toward love.
As long as a muscle or mind can live,
The heart of life has something to give.
Let languid feeling push for the high:
The love, still living, will love what is nigh.
Mayhap, in the time when help seems far,
The soul first turns where the best gains are:
The poor and the sick and the loveless foe
First learn from the humbled what God would
  show.

XXXVII.

Let duty be done, and worth will attend.
Tho' fade each form once called a friend,
Believe, believe Infinity
But thus divides Earth's ministry.
We hear its voice: we know its needs:
We journey toward our separate deeds:
And oh! the further from the world

Life's destined banners be unfurl'd,
We grow, the higher lifts our call,
The less to one, the more to all,
Until, like Christ on the mountain brow,
To God alone we trust our vow.
Ay! there be those so far do soar
    That a single man
    Is lost to the scan,
And the voice of the confident heard no more:
Years! years! when the loveliest face
Seems only a framing wherein to trace
A part of an interest felt in the race.

XXXVIII.

The celibate priest
    Had something to laud,
If nature had ceast,
    Or man were a God.
All things created have need of a sun:
There is no manhood complete but in one.
Watch well! where the highway of life is kept,
However dim by the storms beswept,
The strength of the world is spent in a blast;
The strength of the Spirit appears at the last:
    WE MAY UNITE!
    FOR THE WAYS ARE BRIGHT!

XXXIX.

A-faint in the gloom so rife,
Light! light breaks through! Is it life?
I've seen a face that came, a creation,

A sun, to cluster a constellation
    Of beautiful, bright ideas!
And over the will that slept,
And dream'd of the guard it kept,
There stole the sweetest power to possess,
So like to the Beauty of Holiness,
    Awaking, one had no fears!
Was it something new or something old?
How could it be new, and faith so bold?
How could it be old, and hope not cold?
Or, could it be both? — so dull to the good,
The world waits long to learn what it should:
There is memory far more real than sight;
And state immortal where age is might.

XL.

The years, how slightly they change true life!
We broke for a look, and a whisper of strife:
We said to the seasons: "Come, fold ye between!"
The winters were chill; but the past, it was green.

We called all our passion and pride into might:
We sought for another; none sated the sight:
We push'd through the city: we stroll'd through
    the park:
One spoke in the silence: one moved in the dark.

We dream'd we could mould our being to stone:
Our heart became cold; and our mien became
    one.
God made us for life: a statue we stood:
The surface was smooth; and the world called us
    good.

Oh Marble! what meaneth? These limbs, they
    convulse!
This heart beateth strong! warm floweth the pulse!
The dull ears, they listen! The glaring eyes see!—
Oh Love! so much life, life givest thou me!

XLI.

High, holy Forgiveness, at threshold of bliss
From God in the next world, from mortal in this!
One touch of thy wand, foes, girt to molest,
Drop kneeling, to rise up, knights of the blest.
A current of nature that will can resist
Is check'd, to swell stronger, the longer it's miss'd;
Once fulness of confidence flow'd but in part,
With faith and confession now floods all the heart.

XLII.

Life looks on a face whence beameth bright
A constant halo of warm delight,
    Whose smiles attract
    To genial act
All love that springs in the sunny sight.

Her mien, with every grace refined,
In welcoming, bends to all things kind,
    With something true
    And duteous too,
Not lightly sway'd, in the inner mind.

She moves in a sphere not wholly obscure,
With that which is not wholly mature,

But meek to go
Where friend or foe
May whisper width of the wise or pure.

Her aim is not for prize of a strife,
To sit by a plume, but if as a wife,
    For her own soul,
    Not for eyes of Earth's whole,
Content with gains of the unseen life.

To me like blue that is over the sea
Far up, yet with similarity,
    A world of love
    She bends above,
As broad as life is, and yet how free!

Thence life, bestirr'd, finds fond hopes rise
Like mists, more beauteous when in skies,
    And like nights here
    When stars appear,
E'en gloom grows dear that awaits those eyes.

Ay! thence, as at dawn that awakes a dream,
Hope dims, forestall'd by truth supreme
    That flashes light
    To make all bright,
And be, what self can only seem.

Would God that heaven could ever abide,
Not undisturb'd if storms outvied,
    But steadfast still
    To the clearer will
At rest deep under the wave and tide!

XLIII.

Back! back, Presumption! dare not view
A vision that can but pale the true.
This life hath plenty of wrong for woe:
It need not add one other, I trow:
Nor tempt from the light so bright a soul.
As well a fiend might woo control,
    And drag another to dwell
        In its Hell!—
    Yet oh! a fiend too
    Might aspire for the true!
And if that other were sweet as this,
All fires of Hell were quench'd by a kiss!

XLIV.

In the spheres of God, where Love controls,
Shade hies to the surface; Hell to far poles;
Light bides in the center; Heaven in souls.
'Tis surface-life deems far what's near;
It found no Heaven, if Heaven were here.
This world that weds for elf or pelf,
    Oh it knows not
    What souls have got
That live like God, and, loving, love self.
This world that wisely looks to exalt
Full many another, less spotted of fault,
    It may be right,
    But judges by sight,
Our own is sugar, the others' are salt!

XLV.

Hold, soul! if a freak
But sate as one seek,
God shelter the dream.
Where depth of a stream
Were hid by its gleam,
Agasp on the banks,
The bliss of one's thanks,
The eager bound of one's' leap caused the shock
To kill, as he dived, and dash'd on a rock!

XLVI.

What eye can trace
What is under a face?
If a calm demean
Be of hope serene,
From spirit ascended, through faithfulness,
To dwell in a region above distress;
Or only a stare
From the corpse of care,
From self that is dead but to selfishness?
The genialest glance — Oh trust it never! —
May flare from a passion to scorch forever:
No glory of sky
Where a dawn is nigh;
But flame volcanic that ruins the rest,
That roars beneath and the heaven affronts,
Till one dream of imps that are yelling to pest!
Or wake to the lulls of a soulless dunce!

XLVII.

What seer can pry what cares unfold,
    With children to train,
    And patience to strain,
And after the whim much worth to be doled?
Trust not to feeling, Imperfect of Birth,
Fidelity only has worth on the earth.
    True love's the ideal
Of Faith, that loves most to kneel.

XLVIII.

    Those serpents who visit
    And whisper and hiss it,
    The faithless advice
    Of the first Paradise,
    " Rebellion to station
    Makes Lords of Creation " —
    Oh, who bear the damaging
    Of their sly managing? —
    Ah, how many lone hearts to grieve!
    Vain souls that roam
    From duties of home,
Ye guides unto loving, God's last forms given
At the gateways of Earth, the heralds of
      Heaven,
There's risk where the world's rough cares are
      driven.
    With feeling all ruler,
      The reason is slave:
    With feeling no ruler,
      The female's a knave.

This white of the ermine may prove, forsooth,
A shroud for the delicate beauty of Truth!
Worth lost to get weakness that wins with a lie,
The soul shut in that smothered Love die,
    Weigh well the cheat
    Who look to deceit:
The devil's our rival, ye daughters of Eve:
WE MAY DIVIDE!
FOR THE WAYS ARE WIDE!

XLIX.

Alas Will's boasted freedom! we may!
And have but woe for the murmuring sway!
What soul can hope that a less good here
Shall thrive, with the greatest of all not dear?
The first deed of man with power of selection
    Broke loose from lines
      Of life, all perfection.
His earliest cry: "Who giveth me laws?
    Who leadeth by signs?
      Who telleth no cause?
    The brave hath deserts:
      Let the tree be the quest:
        There is that in the food
      Much more than a test.
    The will that asserts
      Its right of command,
        And calls up the good
        And the evil, shall stand
The equal of God! Have I not desires?
Hail fullness of all their rest requires!"

L.

Alas the finite who aim'd at all sight,
The equal of God is the Infinite!
      And praise to Creator
      In wisdom the greater!
      E'en out of a fall
      Comes the saving of all;
Comes knowledge of good, as well as of bad;
With knowledge of evil from feeling the sad,
The knowledge of faith which alone can unite
Our limit of light to the Infinite.

LI.

Unite! can that be an end, wrought out
E'en through divisions that make Love doubt?—
The width of truths men sunder to own,
Still leading there toward One on the Throne?
Life reads in the past where wish went wrong,
Yes!— even of Love that parted the strong,
Thus to be triumphant!— of Love that was able
To hinder Earth's error, with flood and with Babel;
Of Power, preserving the pure in the ark,
The Father of Faith through the Patriarch,
That led by the meek, that ruled by the poet,
Where Life moved on, tho' no one might know it,
Divided by Egypt, Philistine, and Mede,
That, disciplined, it might learn to succeed!
Moved on! till nigh to a mystery dim,
   Where Thought bow'd awed that a Maker be,
Love crost the threshold; and, knowing of Him,
   Dared e'en to dream of a Trinity!—

No heathen gods of different tale,
But heathen truth where is rent the veil,
    A holy Communion
    Of Heavenly Union,
Of Life in self, and of Life without,
Of Rest, reposing in Rest about,
Of Thought, all knowing and being known,
Perfect of Love that lives not alone,
Of Deeds, whichever their source may be,
All one by an Infinite Sympathy! —
One Spirit ruling on Throne above,
One God, but all of the Godhead, Love!

LII.

And He who rules — One God, perchance,
Has plann'd one law for every advance;
If floods for manhood, baptisms for man,
  Aye parting where sin is, and joining where love,
Each shift but a symbol Faith reads, as it can,
  For growth, not like to the tree forced, above.
For him so ruled, if earth be a school,
May be the life disciplined follows the rule:
Where draw the curtains of pure delight,
The corridors stretch toward Infinite sight:
Love nears through chambers of revelation
The blissful halls of the world's creation:
She beckons to children of Earth, her own
Who wonder and wait, what Faith hath shown;
And the gates flash afar from the Father's Throne
Wherever one gleam of the good before,
Mayhap, an angel opens the door!
Wherever true love, there's faith in the gloom,

A lamp to wait for the World's Bridegroom!
       A lamp to wait,
      Tho' the hours be late
And clear near dawn loom the forms of hate,
For the Judgment Day, the last to divide,
Where the child of Heaven is the fruit of the Bride!
       OF LOVE, TO UNITE!
      WITH THE WAYS ALL BRIGHT!

        LIII.

Hail, Spirit of Union, hail, to control!
       The Bible and Heaven
        These symbols have given:—
One love that joins here body and soul,
And one that joins all Earth to the Whole.
       Who crieth, "Divide"?—
       Love! love it is wide!
Light leads Life on! The haven is near!
Some beacons of peace are glimmering here!
What tho' there be peril, let Faith be devout;
With risk near Eden, there's ruin without!—

Fy! Here is Philosophy, balancing life,
Like the knight of a novel—gone for a wife!

LA.

NOW came the poem of the elder scribe,
　　The village sage, well-nigh the village saint.
Wide seem'd his views, tho' ne'er a voyager; —
For one may see this life and stay at home :
It does not always make men wise, I deem,
That they have napt in Nice, or roam'd 'round Rome :
While many eyes that wander earn but lies,
There's truth in fancy, never found in fact —
As wide too was renown'd his generous worth.
Tho' gray beards could recall a boistrous youth,
And many a scrape and scare from daring deeds,
Who'd now point out, to blame, one earlier blot?
In the completed pictures of this life
Failings may give fill'd outlines rare relief,
A nature weak, in that it was more weak,
By so much more redound to praise of him
Who from poor talents wrought out rich results.
So when the genial man sat at his hearth
To read this work, his wisdom and his worth
First hush'd the throng, and then his clear, full voice,
The wholesome utterance of a well-kept heart!
It spell'd like chiming of the old church bells,
So sweet in youth! 'spite blow and frost, still sweet!

POEM SIXTH.

SERVING.

I.

How sweetly sounds, on barren plain, the rain
   That wakes the slumbering seed that springs to hear!
How bright are steadfast suns that gild the grain
   Ere Autumn crowns with gold the patient Year!
But crystal tones, from infant hearts pure-welling,
   More sweetly rouse the soul's unfolding worth:
And smiles from her whose face lights up the dwelling
More brightly hallow homes for fruit of Heaven on Earth.

II.

So sweet are dawns that bring domestic bliss:
   So bright, the long day's toil that such instills:
Rare rest new cares, to melt before a kiss,
   As slight and brief as snows by southern rills.
And sky-lit, vestal fires at evening glowing:
   All blest the soul to whom one glance allow'd!
Too curst the lone one never, never knowing
That inspiration sent from realms that know no cloud!

III.

What tho' earth's fickle months, with drought and frost,
    Bring most disaster, and bring all distress;
The humblest pair can look past harvests lost,
    Still patient till the future shall redress.
Those youthful forms that grow with careful training
    Bloom beautiful by buds of promised store:
And if this season blast their best attaining,
Oh! has not early prime long years of hope before!

IV.

Thus storms that stalk where man, in vain, contends,
    And crush half ripen'd grain to sudden dross,
Too bitter dross for all more dainty friends,
    Lose power to ruin, and half power to cross.
Let false away, if home's true hearts bide nearest,—
    Privations come, that but deprive of ease;
No loss of other things can seem severest!
Nor any effort tire, achieving still for these!

V.

That one immortal power which ne'er can die,
    There are no floods on earth Love cannot brave,
Too near of nature to the upper sky
    To tamely sink beneath a worldly wave.
And I've known those with all things her expression,

Their wealth, but something won for her to own,
Their poverty, new claim for her confession : —
Ah where could doubtful Fate bespeak so sure a throne!

VI.

A man, whose life had toil'd till nigh its noon
   Through mists which lined each ledge with phantom fears,
Had found so clear a path, so bright a boon.
   High hung the hours through ten full, happy years :
And wide developt joys where Love was wielding.
   Two young hearts came : and with them double care ;
But generous Nature yields afresh to yielding :
The germs that grow to fill feed too on broader air.

VII.

A man, he was — all towns reveal the kind, —
   Earth names eccentric, since Earth finds them few ;
As wise Chinese, with common whisper, mind
   The hang of heathen heads, bereaved of cue.
Of far extremes his nature seem'd the linking :
   Of strong impulses, will outvying all ;
Of reckless fancy, logical of thinking ;
Abstract of reason, still intensely practical.

VIII.

His moods, so wide, in widest fields would roam,
    Wherever love could please, or good exalt;
While Ignorance smiled to feel herself at home,
    And Wisdom would not know he deal'd a fault.
Determined still, he turn'd a fickle bearing,
    Right sensitive, to truth in deed or whim;
A mirror, just and full to each comparing,
Some men there were, to read through what they thought of him.

IX.

Nor here surmise he play'd a gossip's part,
    Or, for a new friend, sacrificed an old.
When one pierced aught to love, one pierced his heart;
    His face grew rigid, for his blood grew cold.
But honor helps us not, if forms have revel'd:
    These moods diverse were doubted and reviled
As scheming, whereat honest hate was level'd;
As aimless, where he'd win, with slight t'offend a child.

X.

His youth, so old, it sometimes seem'd pretence:
    His age was blamed for immaturity.
His foes, astonish'd by his confidence:
    His friends were puzzled by his mystery.
With self diverse, for truth to self ambitious,

His greatest virtue proved his greatest fault:
Ay, men, adepts in vice, had deem'd him vicious,
Because, where Caution call'd, Conceit might fail to halt.

XI.

Alas, 'mid scenes to discipline device,
  Who live, too proud to ply it or too pure,
Will find, at last, they've roused, from lips precise,
Death-scented chidings of the doom'd ill-doer
Who's caught that pest of vice, to sap emotion,
  Who deems a sight of naked heart is sin
And all love haunted by a carnal notion —
So keeps the Christ-like out, to keep the devil in.

XII.

Besides, broad views, alone, have their offence:
  What tho' on life's long voyage loom stars and shoals? —
Both theories for thought, and things for sense?
  One law guides most who steer, where'er their goals:
Who pleads of each to all, may make all wiser,
  But grows no pilot, with his fickle rule!
Nay, ere he know it, 'spite his best adviser,
This man may hear an insult, and that man a fool!

XIII.

Love, when it works a philosophic mind,
  Not long accepts all lack of sympathy:
To seek it kindly, failing still to find,

Makes honest dullness seem hostility.
This man had heart and head so close united,
  All thought was passion, and all passion thought:
Emotion ran to logic, once excited;
And, where the feelings burn'd, Imagination wrought.

XIV.

It wrought his woe: and this his reason knew:
  He knew his own ideals made him sad:
His soul preferr'd to weep and urge the true,
  Than laugh and speak contentment to the bad.
Where did such Romance pace the stage of action,
  One glance from ample perfectness to doff?
The part all spurn'd, she shunn'd by not a fraction,
And then, the pit, which came for pleasure, staid to scoff.

XV.

That modest plant, the schools call sensitive,
  Lacks beauty not when Nature's means are sent:
Its tendrils clasp a harsher guise to give,
  To greet alone some hostile element.
So oft a shrinking mien assumes a boldness
  That masks true life beneath a shield for pain:
But when has pass'd the shade that caused the coldness
Lo! those who watch it well find beauty there again!

XVI.

Thus did the world's hostility, in end,
  See him withdraw ; nor cared he then to live.
But Life that overrules, it rules to blend.
  Who shrink aback meet there the sensitive.
Where honor's scarce and each man craves his
    brother's,
  With such alone are welcome those who feel :
We men are selfish ; and work not for others :
Who've sought it for themselves, have charity to
    deal.

XVII.

Away with shallow precept that extols
  Experience spliced by wedding supplements :
No hearts are join'd, save when, tho' wide the
    poles,
  Life's center's one, for each circumference !
Away with myths, nor quote that silly story
  Of gifts diverse which heirs of jarr'd tastes hold :
For men, much more than man, allure from glory :
Much in the stuff, there's much more in an even
    mould.

XVIII.

He learn'd this truth : that earthly Love can
    wend
  Two ways alone in which 'tis ne'er beguil'd —
Moved forward, pace to pace with like train'd
    friend :
  Moved backward, meeting there each untrain'd
    child.

And when a home had brought both these to-
    gether,
  What rare reward it was for all his care!
It came like summer after wintry weather:
Love touch'd the heart, long dead, for resurrection
    there.

XIX.

But now, in life too bright without a cloud,
  Had the glazed face of Sickness dodged his
    path;
And seized his pulse, first roused to 'scape the
    shroud,
  Then chill'd, by icy touch, to numbness rath.
Friends came; and urged, all other aims displac-
    ing,
  To court the favors of a foreign shore;—
Assured that those far climes, through winds
    more bracing,
Could kindle, once again, the healthful heat of
    yore.

XX.

Both heart and mind demurr'd: he deem'd his
    part,
  At home, a priest of love which lives in form,
True form t'uphold by aught in him of art
  Born in the sunshine or matured in storm.
Again, he thought: "I'll speak, from distant na-
    tions,
  A broader charity from broader glance;
We earthly heralds cannot choose relations,
But, riding on to good, must bridle circumstance."

XXI.

Then pass'd the parting, with its vague regret,
  And dreamlike deeds, and doubtfulness of fact,
The wharf — his wife — his son — his infant pet —
  The long blue hills, slow-failing him who track'd;
And dizzy days; and nights of phantom-fighting;
  And crowded meals which clogg'd an appetite;
And that round waste, without one sail exciting
Monotony too dumb for sentiment or sight.

XXII.

Yet wrong I thee! oh wide and wondrous Strand!
  And those swift wheels which o'er thy surface flee.
I wrong those skies which bend on either hand,
  Lost in the compass of Immensity!
I wrong that mighty heart whose ceaseless grieving
  Wakes wild devotion of the sailor's lays!
That bosom where Omnipotence is breathing!
And, whisper'd from far isles, the heathen's awe-struck praise!

XXIII.

Tremendous Monarch of all Elements,
  Whose broad arms clasp the Heavens, their only peer!

What age of wrong, what wail of Turbulence
  First hail'd thee tyrant of our trembling sphere?
Who bade those Winds upspring, to rouse thy laughter?
  Those Lightnings sport, to cheer thy fretful reign?
That fierce applause to hurry thundering after?
Those Waves to howl and mock above unconscious slain?

XXIV.

Say Power of dread, is it thy rage, or joy,
  Which hurls confusion o'er the Pilot's tract,
And tosses man's proud work, so slight a toy,
  And swamps in spray for each resistive act?
Oh God! protect the soul, those dark mists under,
  Where naught can pierce the veil of instant doom,
Till hidden rock or ice, with madden'd wonder,
Roar at the rising foam, its ghost-track! and its tomb!

XXV.

No human skill saves there! Men work! Men weep!
  Why shouldst thou heed, thou Omnipresent Sea?
Those stormful Clouds, whose blasts about them sweep,
  Owe substance, breath, existence, all to thee!

They gain their grandeur, when thy waves are
    hoary ;
  And when, worn out, their wayward might
    would rest,
Rest shall not come, till thou, with pardoning
    glory,
Shalt gather all again on thy resentless breast!

XXVI.

Nor, when those skies and shores the brightest
    shine,
  Can they outrival thee! oh, Lordly Deep!
Within, and yet not of, that life of thine,
  Behold! more beauteous, all in image sleep!
Ay, Peace, more grandly than when strife is
    raging
  To vex a banishment from wrath sublime,
Crowns thee victorious, every strength containing,
Thou God in miniature! Eternity in Time!

XXVII.

Vain thoughts like these! vain aught which
    spake content!
  Time slowly crawl'd along that endless floor,
Until, one sunny morn, the low lines bent
  On purple downs of Ireland's fertile shore —
That Paradise, beyond the ocean dreary
  Where Neptune sways his lonely dome of
    gray:
Where hung a dream, about the eyelids weary,
More lovely than the hills which circle Queens-
    town Bay?

XXVIII.

Or where could fairy tilt more eager arm
　　Than Spenser spied on those fair banks of
　　　　Lee?
Or how could Beauty spare one other charm
　　Where blithe Kate Kearney sail'd her bonny
　　　　sea?
Isle of delight, and were those gifts expended
　　Of Nature, ere she reach'd the manhood here?
Or was this human filth and misery blended
Lest envy make more jilted, each more jealous
　　　　sphere?

XXIX.

Oh Ireland, Ireland, thou'rt no name divine,
　　Until those earth-bound peasantry are free;
Till Heaven itself shall break those bonds of
　　　　thine
　　And give thee learning! love! and liberty!
Still trim the lamps, tho' voice of hoping falters,
　　The dawn shall come, with all that light insures,
Which long in lands, beside less favor'd altars,
Has nurtured Christian growth from hearts less
　　　　warm than yours!

XXX.

Past leaden Dublin, and her golden bay,
　　The traveler mused on lowly banks of Ern,
And, when the Sabbath came, he paused to pray
　　Where Walker's breath bade palest ashes burn.
Then 'mid the hights that watch'd the Giant's
　　　　ardor,

He traced void walls of coliseums grand;
And heard, o'er sinking ships of Spain's armada,
His wave-swept organ roar an Irish reprimand!

XXXI.

But who, that sought historic mounts and lakes,
   'Trail'd not fair Scotia's image o'er the wave
Toward moles and meads where scarce a sunbeam breaks
   But bounds the ground to star a patriot's grave.
Rare realm of highest deeds! and deepest thinking!
   Honor's delight! and Reason's jubilee!
Where thrives a purer life, pure 'spite the drinking?
Or where does Virtue yearn, it does not yearn for thee?

XXXII.

For thee! and praises evermore a fame
   Where even Vice precedence gives to Worth:
Tho' northern clime may somewhat chill the flame,
   Where Christian zeal illumes the lingering Earth.
For this 'twould fain forgive false virtue's surface —
   Awed by advance of hallow'd Sabbath noons,
Ye beggars, plead no tones but Sunday's service!
Ye organ-monkeys dance no irreligious tunes!

XXXIII.

Who, here, essay to note a stranger's thought?—
  What springs to crowd each path, where'er he turns?
While every course with impulse fresh is fraught,
  Now hale for Wallace! and now hush'd for Burns!
He delved through Bannockburn : he mounted Stirling,
  Full half to Heaven by the view it brought!
Then, all alone, 'mid cliff-wall'd Trosachs whirling,
Was first the stag that shunn'd, and then the James who sought.

XXXIV.

Nor did he slight those tones of tender tale,
  Which murmur where the rills of Yarrow gleam ;
Nor dared one Echo rude alarm the vale,
  Disturbing haunt of Romance and of Dream.
Yet not a limb, nor leaf, above it leaning,
  Nor by its side reclined one sheltering rock
But found a voice with deep poetic meaning,
From Newark's birchen bowers to bare St. Mary's Loch.

XXXV.

Then Cumberland allured, where wilds on high
  Most cultured fruit of earth and mind announce ;

And bright, susceptive Lakes, admiring, vie
   To swell the charms of else unrival'd Mounts.
And sudden brooks whose mists are myths of story
   Dash down each ledge! and dodge through every brake!
From peaks, like broken fragments flung from glory,
Which trail a train of clouds, too like them to forsake!

XXXVI.

And then — vain strove contracted lines of rhyme,
   Describing free orb'd luxury of mind
Our England stirs in souls, of every clime,
   Who honor aught that elevates mankind;
Where grand Cathedrals live! with praises breathing
   Through limbs that yield all graceful wish to thought!
Where classic castles live! with ivy wreathing —
Gardens of freshest art about the ruin sought!

XXXVII.

Vain, too, should Memory seek, through words, surcease,
   Depicting welcome from an English home,
Where no crude Care intrudes on cultured Ease,
   And Service struggles to exalt her own.
God bless thee long, thou proud, but Mother-Nation!

Most motherly in pride, thy sons renew!
God bless that loyal life to each relation,
Bred with the British blood, from lord to tenant through!

XXXVIII.

Thy western child, it grows with noblest boast
　The freedom, first imbibed upon thy knee,
The Anglo-Saxon virtue of thy coast,
　Long stay of Christian life and charity.
And while advancing power fulfills its mission,
　Best culturing all where English words have scope,
Accurst the land, accurst the politician,
Would lift one country's flag to lower the whole world's hope!

XXXIX.

Still slept the snappish gales that fright her waves,
　The while the traveler sought the Belgic shore,
And spires, full-chiming hours each neighbor craves —
　To shun surprise? — a long half hour before.
Well wrought her fields; well her great limner's beauty,
　Tho' skeptics miss that central charm, the heart, —
A wise man's pleasure and a weak man's duty, —
The good which fickle Nature yields to constant Art.

XL.

Art too he found, a cautious, candid school,
   As nicely trimm'd as dikes that guard her homes,
Where crouching Holland grasps her watery tool,
   And tempts to tread-mill each fresh Wind that roams.
So thrift a race, what have they ever slighted?
   In Kirk, behold! what restful industry!
When crowded aisle and organ, loud united,
Praise Him who stretch'd their plains, through long monotony!

XLI.

Not martial pomp, nor splendid choir, we ask,
   Whose end is homage vain to human skill;
No glory to the praise of labor'd task;
   But what, for Nature's mood, speaks out the will: —
Where sense is strong, strong music through the senses
   From souls that love, because they live the strain,
Now slow from doubt, or mourning for offenses,
Anon borne upward wing'd to hope beyond all pain.

XLII.

So grand to hear, where God has school'd by strife,

All powerful chorals from the wills all strong.
Mild moods come too. Our wanderer came to life
Surrounded aye by memories of song
With Heaven-like charm to soothe the child, e'en weaning,
Whose clappers call a roll of classic airs. —
Ah, sweetness sates all earth, when only gleaning
What Germany, replete with growing bounty, spares!

XLIII.

Nor mourn that bounty, ye who'd point to time
Seduced from good by Sunday's beer and ball:
Or mourn each fruit of Eden's matchless prime
For one that rival'd Adam, God and all.
Blest land, indeed, where Conscience bides with Learning,
Considerate still to guard each hour of rest
For man, while man goes wrong and needs, for turning,
Calm hours for view of things Earth's cares cannot suggest:

XLIV.

But well before one blame to bear self-blame:
Where Force of good would hold a stricter rein,
Force may need such from greater need to tame
More blunt and blurting vice of wilder brain.
Where spray is white, waves too are fiercely rolling:

Where Good alert, Ill too, with many a shoal :
Judge not by storm-mood of the mien controlling
The life far less disturb'd where moves a milder
    soul.

XLV.

Or judge and be judged! They've sketch'd : —
    " Play-house, bar,
  Most numerous, crowded, vile and villainous ;
Best stock'd from life where somehow train'd to
    jar,
  Vain girls are rear'd like queens, to reign by
    fuss ;
Whence, void of household joy, man, sot or ser-
    vant,
  From morn to midnight kept from culture's
    part,
Must store, oft steal more gold, that Lies more
    fervent
Greet surface-prink that gilds a home without a
    heart."

XLVI.

No life seems wholly faultless: where not so,
  Let states like souls complete all lack through
    love.
Thus may they lure to Right the Wrong below ;
  Thus, humbly, heed the truth, if Worth above.
That land has kings on earth : — this honors,
    needing,
  Still Sabbaths to remind of King above.

Armies has that: — with this much woe is breed-
    ing
Where Free Will rules, if Will have never learn'd
    of love.

XLVII.

Where'er Republic, thence demands the Earth
    More good to stay a wiser life, in store;
For if the New World be not new in worth,
    The tyrant tracks the circle round once
        more. —
Teach Church, of reverent speech where no
    crown trains it!
    Teach Sunday-school, of love 'mid party strife!
Lest Tyrant-Will, untaught what best restrains it,
Revolt from public peace, or huff the social life.

XLVIII.

Yet, guarding self's, frown not, if Justice find
    All German moods, like music, aim'd for
        heart!
From France some come back Frenchy; but each
    mind,
    More pure of mother-tongue, more self's of
        art,
Comes from this Sister-Saxon, soul-deep nation!
    Ah, if we blame, we'll blame, from loving
        homes
That wait with anxious mien — like revelation,
Words from an oracle! — what speak her mighty
    Tomes!

XLIX.

In all she lack, oh may her new, proud day
  Disclose what facts reveal to heedful thought,
For ends not king-made but what men essay,
  For practice, more than hope, long crush'd, has wrought;
Call impious, Science back, to know her station!
Give sway to Faith! — for there was day, I read,
When not content with whims to guide the nation,
From love of perfect truth, these led to perfect deed!

L.

Across the plains where press'd the Goth and Hun,
  In centuries of progress left in rear,
The pilgrim now was brought with monk and nun,
  To worship art, — and was art only dear? —
Nay, even then, sweet child-like words had mutter'd,
'Spite leading-strings held tight by dotard-hand,
One manly truth, 'mid espionage, still utter'd: —
By dower of soul and hand, the right to speech and land.

LI.

Who made the world, He made the world for man

Where waits he Heaven, with love his only light:
  Its heirs, they cannot bow to caste or clan,
  Be led by aught that does not lead to right.
With such denied, farewell to king or nation:
  The patriot's home is where his duties be!
For priest or prince, love only is salvation!
No rule of heart by hearts without humanity!

LII.

Away with artifice in Church or State,
  Each false result of aristocracy
With good, the say of prelate not of mate,
  With bad, an accident or poverty;
Religion, where the gowning gives the rating,
  Not reverence instinct for life of truth;
Morals, where hopeless virtue yields for sating
The void desires of undomestic soldier-youth.

LIII.

And Hope could prophesy! but spies, far north,
  Foe to free work or worship in her son,
Another cloud! looms it, another Goth
  To out-Rome Rome? to crush all love has won? —
Hail Russia, free! but keep despotic code, ah!
  Hail Europe join'd, indignant then, to fell!
And we — better the smallest rock in Rhoda
Than all the western world, if won through league with Hell!

LIV.

But thou, proud Latin leader, Valor's own,
  Lover — roué of Freedom, France, stand true!
Who has not bow'd, bedazzled at thy throne? —
  Who has not fear'd to hear the Syren too?
Top-wave of fickle-flooding civilization,
  Thy white crests signal winds that work the sea:
Politics, fashion, vice, war, desolation,
Whate'er, where'er the source, each speeds to shape with thee.

LV.

And some forms aid earth much! — Would each crude home
  Grew fill'd with courtesy, the Frenchman's pride:
Would ours so fill'd, that get, o'er ocean foam,
  But modes and words by apes and parrots tried;
While little Soul veils thy soul's true confession
  O'er foreign traits, to make deceit seem right;
And little Learning, needing long expression,
Slights mood-nerved English point, of poem-picturing might.

LVI.

Forgive one, France, if aught of Fashion's tale
  Wake prejudice against thy life unknown.
More moods hast thou than strumpet-signals trail;
  More thought than words thrust, thoughtless, 'mid our own.

True life hast thou: speak for that life addition!
  Shrewd strife to shape needs most a soul-just throne,
Lest logic light like lightning! — smite its mission!
And love with thee seem brightest, since it flare alone!

LVII.

Thus mused, and wrote the traveler, moving on,
  Words tired to trace through what extent of scene.
He mark'd, far south, so beautiful! so wan!
  Fair Spain, nor then forgot what Spain had been.
He heard white Alps preach pearly truths of Heaven:
  Watch'd dizzy cliffs of sober vineyard-glee:
If wisdom came, less weight, perchance, whence given, —
Thought's no aristocrat to need a pedigree!

LVIII.

Yet well to know, where'er his feet may roam,
  America, each son still honors thee,
Where Sect and Sex have found an equal home,
  And Worth ranks first amid nobility;
Where swell the aims of Freedom's humble mothers
  While young minds move toward all that minds deserve;
Where pure the life while Hope, no despot smothers,
Asks but one pride of birth, and God alone to serve!

LIX.

Long, long may tongues diverse and ocean-foam
    Divide the new from modes beyond the sea.
Enough Lies lured where Truth first form'd a home
    Already threaten that which made it free.
Where Nature reigns, let nature seem perfection,
    For truth in bearing, and for love in heart!
For Learning's self a new world! resurrection!
And Heavenlier guise for soul of this earth's wasted Art!

LX.

The wanderer's kin were far, — and Heaven too!
    And oft came letters from the zealous home,
Where Fact and Fancy strove, like marriage true,
    Reflecting bliss, to double every tome.
Right regular they came, till something lured him
    Far Asiatic wildness to explore,
Where mails came not; but ready Hope assured him
More numerous joys would wait more numerous joys in store.

LXI.

Poor vapory life! the Hope died but a Hope.
    The long months pass'd, his eager eyes demand
His letters. 'Mazed they fill so slight a scope
    He opens, reads — but scarce to understand —

Swift tale of stout disease! — how all things
    languish! —
  His two fond children — sicken'd? — dying? —
    dead! —
Then words but blots, steept in a mother's
    anguish;
And then, no more for months! — and God still
    overhead!

LXII.

But last, was note from one, a friend of old;
  On friendship old it dwelt — weak artifice —
Then urged return: "the cause, time would un-
    fold" —
  Return? return? — and needed he advice?
He did return! — And Night! thy self sank fouling
  'Neath mightier darkness there, from shore to
    shore!
And Sea! — in vain obtruded splash and howling!
Woe kept him back from home, alas a home no more.

LXIII.

At length the waves were cross'd: he reach'd
    the land.
  But oh! how different each object here,
Than when, a year before, that little band
  Waved brave farewells upon the fading pier.
No face was nigh to speak a kindly greeting:
  He sought his home — all vacant, cold and
    still:
Wildly the door re-echo'd to his beating:
He seem'd a wicked thing: and slunk back from
    the sill.

LXIV.

His house, it stood beside those lordly Banks
  That rise to greet the Hudson's silvery train,
While Art, admiring, aids, with generous thanks,
  To wreathe still prouder charms for hill and plain.
Below him swept that rare and royal river!
  So white with sails! so restful and so wide!
First of creation, foremost to deliver
To human Skill the power which thwarts the sky-born Tide!

LXV.

It chanced, there was a spot where oft of yore,
  'Neath one broad elm far traced that region through,
He loved to linger, with his babes before,
  And muse on life and all the work to do.
Thither his footsteps turn'd — Too short the story:
  Behold that place of joy! — The same tree waves
Above two little mounds where frost lies hoary,
And him, a lonely man who weeps at silent graves!

LXVI.

And there, in helpless misery did he stay,
  Till twilight came ; till midnight, chill and dim;
And Anguish burst its aching bounds to pray —
  The only thing which life had left for him!
Ay, ay, the only reservoir for sorrow:
  The only outlet for too deep despair:

The only place where hope can find a morrow : —
Oh Father God! oh Christ! oh Spirit, everywhere!

LXVII.

And was he answer'd? — He remember'd, now,
    That friend ; and what was promised to unfold : —
"Where was his wife ?" — he ask'd with pain-braced brow.
    The tale seem'd strange, but very kindly told : —
" A man had come, nigh proved in near relation
    With party foes of his, a well known knave,
Winning her confidence through much persuasion,
Then luring on a speculation wild to brave.

LXVIII.

" Soon, swiftly losing all her husband's gain
    That had been left with her, she went her way,
Searching something to save, — a search in vain :
    While gone, her children died ; return'd, friends say
She first seem'd wild, and then had somewhere wander'd." —
    Such was the tale : it roused one thought : — he must
For her seek all the earth, nor deem aught squander'd
While, all omnipotent, Faith left one hope to trust.

LXIX.

So, on the shifting stage of life appears
    A man, still wedded, but to what is sought,

Still young, if one must reckon life by years,
  But old through care which speeds the pace
    of thought.
Now scans he city crowds, beside him throng-
    ing;
  Now heeds the curious gaze, from village door;
Now dread asylum haunts, with fearful longing;
Now hunts for cautious phrase, to advertise the
    lore.

LXX.

Some whom he met, with words regardful, spoke:
  "Yes, here or there was one, perchance the
    same."
'Twas very kind to cheer the strength of Hope;
  But ah! they never helpt him toward his aim.
But he — no hill so high, it found him tiring;
  No plain so long, the end did not seem nigh.
While glimpsed a single ray to his Inquiring,
The further sank the light, the further would he
    ply.

LXXI.

From east, far west he went; from north, far
    south,
  Led there, at last, he scarcely cared for what:
A change was good: and word, from stranger's
    mouth,
  Might fill the ebbing of a pang forgot.
What courteous homes he met, his mood to
    lighten!
What patriarchal pride of noble clan!

But truth dawns on truth; older right must
    righten:
These too, they lack'd one virtue, to make virtue
    man.

LXXII.

Few can they love who still love manhood best:
    He left for fields, fresh boons of Paradise,
That, slumbering by the Mississippi, rest
    With verdure spurning culture of device.
He left, to be alone, — no wold, no forest,
    Disturbing one long language of repose,
With sateless Beauty's self content as florist,
And only skies where weird mirage and mountain
    grows.

LXXIII.

Then — in the east there lie sky-drifted mounts:
    Their cloud-coursed paths through fresh-found
        mystery,
Dim, dreamy glens, and flash'd surprise of founts
    Had train'd, in youth, his poet-fantasy.
He loved them, as a child may love his mother,
    A simple child who cannot tell you why,
Yet something feels, he feels not for another,
Something too near to life, to need philosophy.

LXXIV.

Thither, from search too vain, his wanderings
    stray;
    And there, in lengthen'd weariness, abide;
While Strength, which stagger'd first, accepts its
    lay;

And Zeal plods on, tho' Zest has stept aside.
The chains our life-experience is wearing
  Goad on to effort, and, through effort, save.
And now, if aught unusual mark'd his bearing,
A lack of it was rest which none but victors brave.

LXXV.

And strong work triumph'd: each new month
  would show
  A milder movement and a firmer eye;
Not as of one who had forgotten woe
  But learn'd to greet expected Agony.
No more sharp pain he felt, so much as sorrow;
  Not some, but all things underneath the shade;
A loss from life which life could never borrow,
But when the lost seem'd God's the gall of grief
  was stay'd.

LXXVI.

One joy too still remain'd. In lonesome time
  Far would he journey, now the soul his end,
Beneath all shape of circumstance and crime,
  To find how Love can ever find a friend. —
Who have not faults? who are not faults regretting?
  Who wish not much? who ever reach their aim?
Who form not plans for all mankind's abetting?
And where in all the deep things are not moods
  the same?

LXXVII.

How then can false misanthropy mislead
  Our younger souls when first they learn of
  woe?

Love is not perfect, oh not so indeed,
    Or Heaven would fail to lure from things below!
But deem no single vice your own strength tasking
    For test, from help and sympathy apart;
The foe may shift attack to different masking,
But all success must pierce the self-same human heart!

LXXVIII.

Go search the world; and, wheresoe'er you stray,
    The wonder is, you find no wonder more.
Behold! the same brisk boys, at wilesome play:
    The same proud mothers, pensive by the door:
The same strong men, bow'd down by weight of troubles:
    The same sad dames, with tired eyes turn'd above:
The same small graves where drop life's bursted bubbles,
Dark most from fear of ill, bright most from wish for love.

LXXIX.

Nor deem, by this cold Unconcern appeals
    To check each special aim of general dust.
'Tis Wisdom's self, for wiser end, reveals
    The heart, and value too, of heart to trust:—
Tho' separate souls, for separate thought, must sever,
    A wondrous oneness in the things most dear;

Substantial want which feels for feeling ever ;
Beneath all selfish sham, a sympathy sincere.

LXXX.

For woe, what is it? — all Complaint that pleads
   Where startled Pity bends in sad surprise?
And bliss, is what? — all gorgeousness of deeds
   That win wide homage from admiring eyes?
Nay! — woe, it is that lonely life's bereaving
   Where threaten'd Hope is nursed in secrecy;
And bliss, it is the glory, or the grieving
Shared with another! — Happiness is harmony!

LXXXI.

A foe, we meet upon a desert plain
   With mutual harmony of wish to part,
Is welcomer than friend who speaks disdain
   To tender utterance of a trusting heart!
Believe you, Christ the Lord had little suffer'd,
   If Woes had made those limbs their only mark —
Ah no! 'twas Love, which felt love undiscover'd!
The Father's face withdrawn! and dying in the dark!

LXXXII.

I dream, when shades which bind the vision here
   Lift in exuberance from a Heavenly view,
All simple shall the grandest truths appear,
   In outlines which, before, all mortals knew.
Let heathen trace aback, through mystic story,
   To lineal loins of Superhuman birth;

The grandest good the Christian knows for glory,
Is simply to inherit, at the last, an earth.

LXXXIII.

An earth, made perfect! — where converting Love
   Should share th' inheritance of all with each!
There generous Bliss, now forced to realms above,
   Would shun no longer individual reach!
For aye, till life be borne to more that blesses,
   Till nature new, perchance, receive new aim,
Who learns to live the true man, he possesses
All things which God who made man like Himself can claim.

LXXXIV.

Toward love, do all who move with right advance
   Through knowledge of the man whom they restore.
The Trade, whose Ignorance crept with lifted lance,
   Has learn'd to feed, unmail'd, each hungry shore.
The Spirit, searching life's full orb of beauty,
   Finds unity 'mid multiformity; —
One soul unseen, the source of varied duty;
With faith in souls unseen; then love to faith's degree.

LXXXV.

Think not I have forgotten him we trace,
   In views which might appear beyond, above.

No truth in sky or earth escapes embrace
  Of aught whose first and last regard is love.
At home in all God's household, naught can sunder
  From God's Infinity, a love-bound soul:
Strong hand in hand it roams with Wish and Wonder,
Till he who sought but one at length have found the whole.

LXXXVI.

How long ere that is found! — fret not to take
  The untried station if beyond the reach:
Accept self where it is, with it to make
  The best result there waiting deed and speech.
'Tis life that brings the rest, oh youthful mother,
  To which you seek to mould your nervous child!
'Tis life, pale boy, you cannot be another!
You try what none can gain! you mourn because beguiled!

LXXXVII.

Long time past on: and, then, one summer eve
  Closed round our wanderer, worn with tramp and heat,
Hard by an inn; — "could its small size receive? —
  Or must he search some distant village street?" —
Such thoughts as these, a moment found him testing,
  Swift through the gate, but lingering on the lawn:

Across the path, like Eden's sword arresting,
From open doors and blinds, a lengthen'd blaze
    was drawn.

LXXXVIII.

"A festive scene! — The stranger here," mused
    he,
  "Were doubly stranger, with my heart of pain."
Then did he stop! and shudder! — was it
    she? —
  No less a thought had roused such blood
    amain.
Convulsed he gazed! Who could have borne it
    mildly? —
  Looks! deeds! and, doubtless, words of love
    were there!
"Is this my wife indeed?" he murmur'd wildly,
"Am I a mortal yet? or have I won despair!"

LXXXIX.

He drew more nigh. — How strong art thou, oh
    Earth!
  How hard the soul must strive that would do
    well!
Our paths divide; the cause, a penny's worth;
  One mounts above; the other sinks toward
    hell. —
There smirking, and behind the bar was sit-
    ting
  She search'd for years — behold Fidelity! —
Gross, vulgar, bloated, face and form emitting
That flush where Flesh revolts from shameful des-
    tiny.

XC.

Her comrade left her with adieu of mirth,
  To ask our wanderer's wish; who answer'd: —
    "life!
Tell me, man, tell — by all your soul is worth! —
  Who? what are you? — and is that — that, your
    wife?" —
The inn-man started back; and then, surveying,
  With a leer laugh of drunkard-wonder, said:
"No jokes, my man, no jokes! — my wife, you're
    saying? —
What, if a bar-maid sport, think you the devil's
    wed?"

XCI.

"Devil!" he gasp'd; then turn'd, nor more in-
    quired:
  He did not look behind, nor look aside:
His tottering limbs, oh! they were very tired! —
  A beggar stopt to spurn such lack of pride.
"Think you the devil's wed?" one heard him
    sighing,
  As tho' 'twas all he thought about, for days:
"Wed! oh not wed," he groan'd "that's loos'd
    at dying:"
And death would seem to come; but harsh life
    woke the haze.

XCII.

Full clouds may empty soon: he found it so:
  And bow'd, but as an oak before the blast:

Something is shaken off; but more will grow:
   And life is stronger, when the storm is pass'd.
Strange it may seem, but there is being, younger
   From chafing much through blows of blustering sway. —
Desires, uncloy'd, for simplest sunbeams hunger:
And live unrest contracts no mildew of decay.

XCIII.

He was not one to pause where questions win:
   And where did ample gossip fail the spell? —
"Ah yes! the inn was known; and all within:
   Full many a sober man who went there fell.
The woman" — here they shrugg'd — "not too much squander'd
   Of worth in her, for him, they guess'd, or them.
She mixt not with the village: and they wander'd
Not far to seek her: — where's no glimmer, there's no gem."

XCIV.

"Facts, facts?" he ask'd; as tho' the unseen truth
   Had mystery which could awe those social ways
With charity right orthodox, forsooth,
   And vice or virtue, self neglect or praise.
Facts found he none; so turn'd, with wiser scheming,
   To wait, self-crown'd, an angel of defense,

Moved but for her; he might be her redeeming:
And tho' all else might doubt, he pray'd for confidence.

XCV.

He sought, and braved well, all there was to hear;
   As if, for her, his suffering could atone;
Then, once, in place where others were not near,
   Again he met her, face to face, alone.
Wild was she first, with eyes whence hate was beaming;
   Then pale became, too pale for his alarm!
There was a sigh! a fall! no more of seeming:
Nature had conquer'd both! he raised her on his arm.

XCVI.

Long was it ere he roused her from her swoon:
   And longer ere he calm'd affrighted blood.
Then, when thought came, came groans to wake too soon,
   A wish for death, and words, a muddled flood
Pleading for pardon; but, in end, more clearly
   Told long derangement; then, with calmer voice:—
"I would win back your gold; I paid too dearly;
I delved too low, till shame, it left no other choice."

XCVII.

"Too much of choice," he thought, "God curse the claim!"—

Then, waiting long: — "How hard it is to
    win!" —
And Mercy high bestow'd a kindlier aim,
    To balance long intent 'gainst sudden sin. —
"Nay," said he, "Memory, it shall blot forever
    This latter tale; and read but earlier life.
Trust to my care again; naught, naught can sever
The souls whom God has join'd: come back; you are my wife."

XCVIII.

A moment, 'spite of misery, she smiled.
    Then, suddenly, "Nay!" she exclaimed, "Nay! nay!
Oh never shall your home be thus defiled! —
    Think, think how I am changed! — what Earth may say!"
Again he paused. — Forgive, he was not stronger:
    Truth halts just where too ready Falsehood hies: —
He feels the truth too well, and feels it longer;
Altho', with mien becalm'd, he calmly thus replies:

XCIX.

"What man may do, or say? — In younger years
    There was a time, this test was all to me.
On Earth, I sought my goal, my hopes, my fears;
    But could not find the whole I long'd to see.
There came another day: my soul look'd higher,

To seek in Heaven what it miss'd in Earth:
And blest therein; but could not aye aspire;
And when I gazed around again, I knew of dearth.

C.

"There may be those whose feelings seem unwise:
   I deem'd mine had a cause, — some fault, near by.
Then would I pray; then, pledged to effort, rise
   As tho' impatient work could satisfy.
Last, He who has, 'spite all that priests have doubted,
   A human way of answering every soul,
Sent you, with purpose their false creeds have scouted,
To match my partial life; and make my manhood whole.

CI.

"What was there then which you were not to me? —
   Blest as a messenger from Good above,
You brought me bliss: you bade my misery flee:
   You were a focus for all light of love:
And, by that light, did purity gain whiteness:
   And aims, you deem I cherish, what could cheer:
Ay, ay, from you, earth gather'd all its brightness!
And through your soul I look'd to find the Heaven dear!

CII.

"And that I shall forget this past, think you?
    Shall life forget itself? — shade lighter sin
By suicide? — oh, trust me, Griefs pursue,
    As jockeys scourge, — to make the whipt steed win!
Behind, then, let us leave but things that smarted!
    Keep love alone, and nothing can be loss!
Who looks beyond, 'mid wind and wave, true-hearted,
These seas of woe wreck not! they speed his power to cross!"

CIII.

He waited; then, with troubled heart, once more:
    "Come," said he, "we will seek Love's only throne." —
And peace came, such as meets you, at the door,
    Oh world-wide wanderer, of a world unknown!
He pray'd for perfect love, with thought related
    First time in long, long seasons not alone;
Nor age that drank from youth was quickly sated;
But when he'd ceast, behold! the cause of hope was gone!

CIV.

And where was she? — The slow days cross'd the hills:

The loud storms rose, and fell, and rose again:
And there was search anew, which naught fulfills:
And all was done, till all proved done in vain.
At length, the third month brought with it a letter,
Writ by a kindly doctor, known of yore,
"She had been ill," he wrote, "but, now, 'twas better:
Hers was that quiet home which Earth disturbs no more."

CV.

A final charge, she left: — "Untrammel'd still" —
Her words were quoted — "live, with promise high:
Claims there are, broader than our narrow will:
Far better we should part now, you and I.
For me, await dear children with no mother;
And oh, so much I need to have reveal'd:
There shall my poor life's failure vex no other:
And there, God grant! at last, I'll look where all are heal'd.

CVI.

"For you, oh Husband, lingers better fate; —
Gain in this sphere, and gain in spheres to come;
Good, summon'd long, equipping through the state,
And greater good, beyond Earth's battle drum.

Was I life's light? — That middle light was
    given,
  When young, too young for truth mature to
    cheer:
When old, what curse, tho' nothing's bright but
    Heaven?—
Farewell: with lives apart, but love forever
    near."—

CVII.

My tale is told: if ye whose eyes it meet
  Deem it a simple tale, so let it be:
And think, once more, how many on the street
  Have lips, could tell a simple history!—
If ye have needed no experience ruder
  To crush a confidence of long complaint,
Give thanks! To one thus minded, life's Intruder,
With blows that come to thresh, may winnow but
    the saint.

CVIII.

And would ye seek him whom these lines portray,
  Deem not his ways to mournful moods adjust.
Ah no! Life bringeth too a brighter day:
  Naught harms the soul, that does not harm
    its trust.
For him, who still has faith for generous action,
  Full many a thankful eye bespeaks success;
Full many a thought that thrills the nobler faction;
Full many a social sphere that circles wide to
    bless.

CIX.

The years speed on. He early toils and late;
    Nor dreams he every gain from times to come:
Oh, is not good equipping through the state?
    And is a useful life, a martyrdom? —
There are no tones from loving hearts now welling,
    No faces, now, to cheer his lonely hearth;
But there are smiles, from source above dispelling,
And all that is most bright, it comes from Heaven not Earth.

SI.

O'ER life of the first poem years had past,
　　Few years, yet in those few had grown a man
The young store-clerk whose pen had further'd it.
For those years had compress'd in pressing times
So many long days' toils that took but one,
So many friendships form'd in forming camps,
So many crowded tramps toward victory,
So many honors gain'd through single deeds,
So many funerals for Faith to face,
So many lonely tears of suffering,
So much of Lie doom'd to eternal death,
So much of Truth saved for eternal prime,
That many a sire of threescore years and ten
Told them, might weep his own as half a life!
Nor had the brave youth left that sea of war,
Those stormy blasts, and death 'mid fire and wreck,
For mildly murmuring rills of rhyme again,
Ere the loud waves still roaring roar'd alone
To bid all heed how near, how dear the port!
But then, with wounded limb, at home once more,
With joy he'd join'd the poet in his praise, —
Praise in the dawning of a coming peace,
A song, not chirping low 'mid doubtful dusk,
But lark's-like, trembling where to rest were heaven!

POEM SEVENTH.

WATCHING.

I.

LIFE is one, whate'er the portion; ease to play, or toil to plan,
Joy or sorrow, haste or caution, all must blend to make the man:
Youth to fail or age to prosper; both to sink beneath a blow;
God is greater than disaster: life is one, not all below.
It is one tho' lives be many; good or bad may rise or fall;
Honor droop, or treason flourish; Love that righteth, righteth all.
Trust no greatness with a greater: man is strong, but God is strength:
And the breath of the Creator wakes the dead to win at length.
Howsoever lone the contest, do not dream Good moves apart:
Mixt and hostile seem the summons; one has only known the start:
There's a blast whose sound is louder than an earthly trumpet-call:

In the end beyond each other, God alone is all in
    all.
Life is one for stars or spirits! from the oceans to
    the fires;
From the righteous blaze of Heaven to the gloom
    where Wrong expires.
Trust the grandeur of disorder, and a grander Will
    to blend,
God!. the Alpha and Omega, the Beginning and
    the End!

II.

Happy he whose steps can wander o'er the smoke
    of present strife,
And, above distraction, ponder all the far results
    of life:
Be he soldier, sage, or poet, it is he whose views
    sublime
From that hight of central wisdom guide the cir-
    cling shifts of Time.
Just as blest the humbler toiler who beneath, in
    battle black,
Hearing voice of Truth Eternal, thence perceives
    the foe fall back:
He as well with thankful spirit, 'mid successes
    swift tho' late,
Learns to know the Source of victory; learning
    this, learns too to wait.

III.

He shall find life not all law: in nature, things
    not seen to grow;—

Storms that slip the bars of sunshine! meteors
that strike fire through snow!
Thought that is not led by Logic! Proof that
leaps the lines to show
How the breath of Truth is stronger than the
beatings of its foe!
There are mild Words that can waken fear! and
struggle! and despair!
Tho' they leave no track behind them; nor a
shade to mar the air;
Do not glitter in the sunshine; do not thunder
o'er the plain;
Do not flash' the leaden lightning; crowd no
clouds to shroud the slain:—
Words of Truth and Words of Godhead! Words of
Christ! and every where
When they sound the Lies that lurk in forms possess'd of evil there
Rend mistaken frames that held them! leave each
writhing on the ground!
Skulk aback to native darkness! sink below to
woe profound!

IV.

In the course of men and nations, there are times
that are not blest,
When the surface seems the substance, and forgot
is all the rest:
As the life is, so the thought is; depth unsounded,
truth in doubt,
Groping men who touch each other learn to leave
the spirit out.

Clouds hang earthward; and they nod, 'mid dreams
    that Heaven too is low:
And they kiss the dust, half-hoping God. an idol,
    worshipt so.
Then comes need of revelation; and the Truth
    that dwells above
Sends the Light in ways that publish both its person and its love:
'Mid the gloom the sun-bright chariot dawns and
    glances through the air,
And the cheer of Faith awakens, just as most
    await Despair.

v.

Weaker souls who kneel to error, what are we to
    weep the truth,
Cowards for another's vigor, laggards for another's
    youth?
Why should private gage a conflict by his danger
    or degree?
Wherefore fret impatient projects for an end he
    should not see?
In the work we have before us, what are we that
    we should live? —
Proud indeed to be permitted feeble succor still to
    give:
Yet the poor man from his cottage, and the rich
    man from his hall
Here fill equal spheres, the agents of the Lord
    who doeth all.

VI.

Trust! altho' the tyrant prosper: 'tis the triumph of the Wrong
Is its own tribunal! Patience! heed the plea, and watch the throng.
You shall find in wrong more error than can make the wish unkind:
When its spring is not the clearest, not the clearest all the mind.
Working out through thought and action, wrong would earn an ill surcease,
E'en tho' righteous Indignation ne'er did break a guilty peace;
E'en tho' Evil, grown presumptuous, did not force the test of power,
Blow with madden'd lips the summons of its own worst fated hour;
When, amid confusion thronging, comes stern Opportunity,
Sworn to punish for the present, proud to maim eternally! —
Who, with test of arbitration once submitted to the Lord,
From one deed, His Love condemneth, dare withhold the lifted sword? —
Oh! I hail the crackling barriers of expedient compromise,
Pledge to Error that forswears them! let them fall that Right may rise!
And I welcome on the war-cry when the true together run! —

Hosts in Heaven seek truth together, every step and impulse one.
It is Christ-like, God-like, dying for another's liberty!
Live or die, with right remaining, God remains! — and victory!

VII.

Even so, the Lord hath triumph'd. High and wide, on hill and heath,
Sprung and flash'd the sword long rusted, then, made bright, return'd to sheath.
Friends, forgive too wild emotion. If the old man's joy appear,
Let the truth, forever young, rejuvenate a frosted year!
'Tis not oft, the few souls searching Freedom, wandering in its youth
Through the dim and direful pathways that ensnare the child of Truth,
Have so soon, amid their doubting, found among their little band
That unknown One, girded, silent, but immortal to command;
Or have seen their flickering torches pass'd along through all the dark;
Or have heard their own weak summons echoed loud from wild and park:
Therefore, let us joy and worship: glory to the Lord and praise!
To the lost he brings salvation! light illumines all the ways!

VIII.

Am I wrong? — Oh say some prophet? must I speak no Heavenly plan?
Tune, like Miriam, no praises for deliverance that I scan?
Trace I not the Spirit's leading, wheresoe'er a slave 's made free?
Or a free race threaten'd have maintain'd the cause of liberty?
Or is then that watchword rousing every age and every van,
Liberty! a lying instinct from the God who made the man? —
Nay, I err not: Ill, there present, banish'd Adam; outlaw'd Cain;
Cheer'd and cringed to Saul's oppression; went, led captive o'er the plain:
'Gainst the Ill, Life moves to action, sway'd by words of Prophecy: —
That "the bonds shall all be broken, and the captives shall go free;"
Faithful still to Him who governs Heaven, and Earth, and age, and youth,
Saints in rest, and men in motion, and the unity of Truth!

IX.

There be those who limit promise to this smaller, earthly ball: —
Life is one: on earth is but a germ, tho' still a germ of all.

There be more who limit virtue to a place where
    all is bliss : —
Life is one: the right in that life is the flower of
    right in this.
Let me never aim for FREEDOM, careless of one
    conscious chain :
Law is one; and Love appealing points to all
    woes that remain.

X.

I am old : my sleep is troubled ; and the course
    of daily Thought,
Plunging into darkness, peoples all the night with
    what it sought :
And, as weary eyelids close, to ope in realm of
    visions rare,
It may be old age is childish ; yet I watch and
    wonder there !

XI.

Once, I found a mortal struggling toward a lone
    isle of the sea,
That, in such, no other's Will might breathe a threat
    to Liberty :
First came peace ; but soon vain Fancy that had
    fought each rival's tone,
Occupationless and restless, stirr'd revolt to Reason's throne :
Mock'd the winds like human voices ! moved the
    shades like human forms !
And the leaves, like footsteps, rustled 'twixt the
    thunders and the storms !

While the cynic, far from manhood, what was manhood's self forgot,
Curst the earth, and curst the heaven; rest or freedom had he not.

XII.

Then I saw a wiser instinct flowing forth unitedly,
Where far people flock'd together at the cry of
  "Liberty!"
'Twas like thunder to the hill-sides, shaking seas
  from every spring;
Roll'd like waves upon the ocean when the sailors
  cease to cling;
Till the mighty surf, swept onward, quench'd be-
  neath its hissing tide
All the flaming guns that bellow'd from the towers
  of tyrant-pride!
Crash'd the walls with dread resounding! — but
  the weary waters sank: —
Fickle flood! — where fell the ruin, rose a stouter,
  stonier bank.

XIII.

Then appear'd wise lords who ponder'd: — "Men
  with diverse wills to blend,
Men grow mad: let one be master; let the dream
  of poets end."
Spake they truth, or spake they error? — sift the
  bran of heresy:
Part is truth to tempt the cautious; part is lie to
  poison by. —
Truth or error, God had granted Saul but at the
  people's choice;

Grants Oppression — ne'er till cowards whimper for
 a braver voice.

XIV.

Oh, ye statesmen, sages, soldiers, ye who watch
 the range of sight,
Ye do well to name things "dreaming" which Philosophy calls "right!"
Dreams they are, for in our doing each one grasps
 the gains of earth,
Selfish here, and there suspicious, cursing down his
 brother's worth;
Each a tyrant of his corn-field, fencing up the last
 by-path,
Whining out for laws t'uphold him, and restrain the
 neighbors' wrath.
Man's own self it is that limits all the good that
 might be his:
His own heart whose fears and failings keep the
 soul aback from bliss;
While his Wish would injure Love, just Conscience
 holds the Wish confined:
And the statutes are the mirrors of the slave within
 the mind.

XV.

Yes! we need that Earth grow wiser, ere prepared
 to have the true;
Thought for common weal to rule us, ere the lines
 of law be few;
That some Light from out the Heaven dissipate false
 shades of fear,

Ere we spy the worth of manhood, and how much in souls is dear;
And, above all, that which only can give true equality,
Views of God, that in His presence human greatness cease to be!

XVI.

Far above, I saw a Monarch, with a glory like the sun,
And like stars his loyal subjects, for all brightness sprang from one:
Where they moved, with His will prompting, came no check:—but one could see
Every path, which lay wide open, led along Infinity.
Plenty ripen'd there for all men, springs of joy, forever quaft,
And their depths, which lost no ripple, closed above the largest draft.
Then the people, earth's sad people, far without that realm of light,
Crush'd by burdens, sinking prostrate, this was that which lured their sight;
This was that which from the distance roused their cheer for "Liberty!"
Right to deem it all of Heaven! God! and dearest destiny!

XVII.

Once, amid dread Sinai's wonders, through thick clouds and tempests driven,
Came the Vision to the prophet, speaking changeless laws of Heaven.
Earth with all of Israel trembled, yet those whom these laws restrain'd,

Hearing truths, long vaguely guiding, knew 'twas
    Love had all explain'd :
And the wise adored a standard, clear beyond all
    sophistry
King or priest, with blinded conscience, to inter-
    pret wrongfully.

XVIII.

Once again was law explain'd, the mystery of its
    source and end,
When the Sovereign Love appear'd, a man to follow
    as a friend,
For the letter'd law the Spirit, Life to lure, through
    truth shown dear,
Souls unconscious of constraining, from all goading
    conscience clear.
Law remains! but law's fulfillment, it can hush
    earth's long complaint :
It is love for all of duty, moves oblivious of restraint.
Till such come shall bonds protest against the
    crimes they would restore :
Only Love can sway the land, yet open every prison
    door : —
Self shall stir, 'mid jealous rulers, false aggression,
    falser pride :
Only Love can govern justly where the wrongs of
    race subside.

XIX.

Joy it is, to know in all things that the deeds
    which seem our own,
Struggling on to grand achievement, are not left to
    move alone.

All true living seems a circle, curving with mysterious cord
Up through wish and out through action, sweeping from and to the Lord.
In the soul's profoundest being, when all worldly strife is still,
Flames a power from inspiration, lighting the reluctant will:
And the man who, in thick darkness, gropes to find a better day,
By the red fire of his spirit reads some signals of the way:
Nor pursues mere flash and shadow! Oh! to those who still aspire
Comes a Word, a Light, dispelling dim delusions of desire.
Happy he to whose ideal real good the spectacle,
For the only holy aim must be the highest possible!
When the Spirit's loving moves us, and the mist 'fore Truth dissolves,
Safe within a mystic orbit, doubly blest our course revolves.
Then the Faith that waver'd looks back, restful, on the Infinite:
Then the Hope, with eyes a-vacant, spies the Beatific Light!
Here is life's completed cycle! here the long lost harmony!
Here awakes the soul's dear music! here the bliss we pray shall be!
Out of it, the charm is broken, tangent-jarr'd to lone dismay. —

Heaven, preserve us all from straying, guide our
    wish, and guide our way!
Match again the lost connection where creation's
    currents blend,
God, the Alpha and Omega! the Beginning and the
    End!

xx.

As in one life, so in many: no high purpose
    prompts a race,
But above, some Revelation moves the headlights on
    apace:
No forsaken germ is progress, growing from inhe-
    rent powers,
But a trunk, ofttimes ingrafted, touch'd from Heaven,
    aside from showers.
It was when God walk'd with fathers, that the sire
    was king and seer;
When He spake from Sinai, then were oracles, and
    priests, and fear:
With the later, ampler truth, revealing loyalty as love,
Freedom grew a faith and flourish'd, nurtur'd by
    the skies above.

xxi.

And my soul has thought that Wisdom, tracing
    back the mighty plan,
Might not scan in all of history more than marks
    the single man:—
When the weakness of the infant first assays an
    appetite,
Then maternal care that nurses finds the way, and
    names the right:

When the child has grown to manhood, looking toward Eternity,
Rule and reason both must guide him toward a self-wrought destiny.
There was age, in Earth's beginning, when the mind, which solved no cause,
Knelt in reverence to commandment, and to holy text of laws:
Comes an age, as Earth grows older, when the soul, 'mid wider light,
Grasps the wonders of creation, and the wisdom of the right:
God is Lord through independence! Truth and Error, equally,
Lure Experience into danger, that it learn humility:
At the last shall Faith triumphant, freed for worthier worship, bend,
Taught to know Who is Omega, Who Beginning, Who the End!

XXII.

Who are they whose deeds shall stand, the monuments to mark their time?—
Deeds of those who build with God, a structure strong for endless prime:
All beside, with heat and bluster, splendid scaffolds only rear,
Doom'd to fall, 'mid waste and wonder, when the unseen towers appear.

XXIII.

Well for earth did zealous leaders plan but to fulfill the Word,

That "the kingdoms of the earth shall be the kingdoms of the Lord."
Oh the Times might bound right onward: there are lights all down the track:
Yawning brakemen fear for darkness; and we jolt with war and wrack.
Oh for power to rouse their torpor with a draft of heavenly health!
Oh for power to show the stations, gleaming far with waiting wealth!
Thanks to God, our ways are weakness: there is something wiser still
In the steady wheels of progress than within a human will.
Heaven, it is, controls the sunlight that shall wake each selfish dream;
And reveal to guilty slumber, good is nearer than may seem.

XXIV.

Hark! e'en now the wind a-whisper! and the men of active heart
Spring to bear glad tidings forward, ere the day is seen to start.
What to them is wild or ocean, care or loss, disease or death?
What are thorns that vex the body to a life that lives in breath?
Lo! by stranger-ears unheeded, long they cull from ancient tome
Words to worthily speak out the worth of Truth to heathen home.

But alas for lengthen'd effort! what, to stupor,
    choicest words?
Deep-brought thought to superstition? soul-sent
    eloquence to herds?
Oft in distant fields, 'mid shadows slowly lifting,
    one by one,
Doubt on empty nest sits brooding o'er the things
    that have been done.

XXV.

Note again! the light advances! men, uprising
    o'er the plain,
Spy along the far horizon broader fields for broader
    gain.
Comes a wind of wider wielding: wakes a flutter
    o'er the strand:
All the banners white of commerce pushing out-
    ward from the land:
Stirs again a sound of struggle: wheels that beat
    the thwarted main;
Willful wheels that mount the mountain; and that
    leap the lonely plain:
Nerve-like wires that whiz and wander; light that's
    burning through the sea;
Earth's united orb electric to one touch of sympathy!
Look! long hosts of emigration, sweeping on with
    golden train,
Wonder, worship, imitation,— harvests on the desert
    plain.
Knowledge, Virtue, Wisdom come. Oh toil ye on,
    ye mission-souls!
Deeds are grander than Earth's planning: It is
    God who still controls!

Move thou on, bright Sun of Morning: burn the mists upon the hills:
Flame against the frozen summits: flash adown from melting rills:
Thaw the whited wastes above us: flood the plains to culture Worth:
Rout the clouds, and leave but Heav'n 'twixt man and God who gave him birth!

XXVI.

Now comes day, that better dawning, when, from glance of waking eyes,
Flit the dreams of present progress, pale their pageantries of lies.
Come divines, and search the outlines of a sect that had a fame:
Feel for phantom of the darkness: love is left without a name —
Freer forms and more of feeling; less of talk and more of deed —
What the Bible leaves to manhood, leaving to the souls who read.
Statesmen, come, and search the limits of a nation fear'd of yore:
Clearer now the light beyond you: lo! the shadows fold no more.
Where those far, mysterious murmurs, movements of a dusky race?
Where are they? Who find the stranger meet the God-like face to face.
More and more give way the barriers: one of feeling, one of thought, —

What is there to hinder all things that the strug-
    gling world has sought?
What are plains and mounts and oceans, what are
    tongues to unity?
Commerce, customs, institutions, have not all one
    destiny? —
When the time comes, righten evil, spite the selfish
    or the strong,
Gog and Magog or the devil, — or conservers of
    the wrong!
When the time comes, there's a banner by the right
    to be unfurl'd
Where the patriot of the nation stands the patriot
    of the world!
When the time comes, there's a Babel where shall
    sound one Master-call,
And the people mount to Heaven, with the Lord
    there, all in all!

XXVII.

When the time comes, ah! that future! blessed be
    the eyes that see —
Ay, and blessed they who hope it, free from earthly
    tyranny,
From the world whose calmest living must be one
    long struggle here
'Gainst the moulds that strain and shatter all that
    Nature's child held dear!
It shall need no simple logic, to reveal that rage
    of kings
Holds no calmer rein to war than slaves who
    bear its sufferings;

Or to waken trust, where God gives wish for freest
    thought and speech,
That the right is meant to prosper through a true
    regard for each.
Long as anxious Progress lingers by the gate, with-
    out the keys,
Vain attempt for equal love until the proud sur-
    render these.
You shall find each older bigot sway the younger
    statesmen's skill,
Grinding lesser wheels the closer, smooth to work
    the monarch's will:
While there's dirty work to forward, speaking:—
    "Ignorance for the worst:
Shut away the light of learning, lest they learn
    themselves accurst:"
Long as fills the purse of Empire:—"Pet police
    and veteran;
Crush the grape, the more's the yielding; better
    money than the man:"
If the wiser conscience question:—"Oh! the
    priest's ordain'd to rule!
What, tho' meant for darker ages?—for the forms,
    preserve the fool!"

XXVIII.

Where oh, where shall faith in broader honor to
    outweigh the small,
Outweigh individual scheming, by intrusting power
    to all?
Where shall states, with generous welcome, bidding
    all ambition rise,

. Press around the growing infant truth to make
    each ruler wise?
Where shall Virtue seeking comrades, Worth the soul
    to breathe through speech,
Learn to prize a loftier level where all hope
    exalteth each?
Truth! the Infinite! the All! that rules through
    finite thoughts of man,
Where shall it be sought and follow'd through the
    laws that all shall plan?—

XXIX.

Lo! there dawn'd a light about me: and a vision
    in my sleep
Rose above the midnight vapors, and it floated o'er
    the deep:—
Shell of alabaster brightness by an unseen impulse
    drawn,
Speeding on three forms who journey'd softly as
    the sprites of dawn:
Beauteous stood the central figure, with her mild eyes
    on the sky,
But with prayerful frame bent forward, eager, as
    for large reply:
Just above her unbound ringlets, seem'd to gleam
    the morning star;
And within her burnish'd breastplate, mirror'd
    lands to glance from far:
'Neath her left hand, turn'd averted, crouch'd the
    aged limbs of War,
Yet he clutch'd his lightning-quiver, fierce as
    youngest conqueror;

While, from harsh face gazing backward, wild his
 red eyes flared to see
Dark Confusion linger slumbering on the limits of
 the lea :
At her right hand, closely clasping, knelt the white-
 robed form of Peace,
As a prince might kneel for crowning, or a saint
 before release ;
With her free hand at her forehead, shielding the
 intenser glance
Of a face that still spake : — " Patience ! " yet for
 ever spake : — " Advance ! "
Where they moved, bright shapes before them sprang
 from out the sky and sea —
All the golden Hopes of Heaven leaping to live
 Prophecy !
'Twas as though a grander nation, wash'd of preju-
 dice and pride,
Past a newer, broader Jordan, rose upon a brighter
 side —
'Twas a world that caught a glory, flash'd along
 from mount and isle —
'Twas the Heaven itself unfolding where all nations
 throng'd the while —
And a young Wind rose that whisper'd : — " Where
 shall man to man be true ? —
With The Old is hard repentance ! Freedom hies
 to seek The New ! "

XXX.

" To The New ! " — I caught the accents ; and I
 gloried in the theme :

And I shouted it in slumber, so the cry awoke my dream.
Then I found me old and feeble, faint, with so much work to do,
"Ah!" I moan'd:—"All things that falter,— what can live but in The New?"

XXXI.

Oh, ye newer, truer Hearts, that beat in fresher ranks of life,
Youth, brave youth, the cheer of present, and the strength of future strife;
Forms, whose steps are recreation, and whose very breath a joy,
All unwearied from the pathways where this smoke and dust annoy;
Faces, bright to coming fortune, beauteous in the flush of zeal,
Fixt and frosted not by winters that have chill'd first faith in weal;
Eyes, that proudly dodge contentment, free of welcome for the strange,
Not yet cower'd by cruel blows, nor disappointed past a change;
Souls, that ne'er have cring'd to failure, or surrender'd flag of hope,
But adown life's longest vista spy the Heaven, its only scope;
Do you know how tired Age rallies when it hears your bounding tread?
How in your endearing presence every weaker Love has fled?—

Age! — I see the angels bending through this thick
 and troubled air! —
Ah, fair spirits, fresh from Heaven, without you,
 life were despair!

XXXII.

Thanks to God, Life moves on with you! Time,
 that rides to victory,
Thunders past the fainting soldier, rousing thought
 of what shall be.
So is Hope triumphant ever! Life has had its fill
 of pain;
But the shade of Melancholy claspt me to her
 breast in vain.
Phantom film of mortal making! — what was she
 to hide the Heaven?
My weak hands that clutch'd despairing, as they
 stirr'd, beheld her driven.
If there be one woe more dread in fabled realm
 where dawns no day,
Where the nearing fumes of torment choke the
 laughter of the way,
Where the greedy fires before one tear swift drafts
 from all the air,
Till, like brute that bounds toward burning, sense
 be fever'd to despair,
It is that, to him who seeks it, turning back from
 reckless fear,
All the flames light up no outlines of a hope, of
 old, so dear.

XXXIII.

Never, while these years are waiting larger earthly waste of man,
With the strife for Heaven still raging, does the dark hide all the van.
Howe'er thick the gloom have gather'd, howe'er fierce the missils be,
Through the Thunder's trembling pathway glimmers light for victory!
All above us, all about us, rift the clouds from prospects still,
Aims of Hope that e'er abides to marshal on the loyal will?

XXXIV.

Aims of Hope that moves to triumph! triumph, not alone for youth,
But for age, for all who worship immortality in Truth.
Far above the under effort, which these troubled ages know,
Scans that wiser Trust that tells us: — life is one; not all below.
Where does Meditation ponder, Sorrow fold a whiter shroud,
Conscious not of blessings nearer than through Time's long battle cloud?
Fancy, flying to her mission, shoots along the starry way:
Reason follows on, beholding wider bliss the more they stray:

Both, with growing light bewilder'd, down to darkness fall — in vain!
Only wise in wishing wisdom! failing but to fail again!
Still would Logic hold its centre; still the Conscience claim its throne;
Age await the gates of Heaven; and the soul maintain its own;
All the loss of lower living trust to higher destiny,
Even tho' no Revelation made them all a certainty.

XXXV.

Ne'er can mortal wing his vision up within those bright abodes;
Ne'er can breathe that air seraphic; ne'er can touch those shining robes;
Ne'er can press that hand, grown sacred from the heart whose work it plies;
Ne'er can watch the light of Heaven in those peaceful soul-lit eyes;
Ne'er can list to sweetest music, spell, where hush the angel-wings,
Weird through mild, unconscious pathos which dim-dying memory brings:
Never human foot has journey'd o'er that dark and long abyss,
Toward where hearts, new-nerved by loving, thrill the pulse to endless bliss:
Seldom saintly guest has blest us down amid these vales below;

Or, inspired by recollection, read a requiem to woe:
Still we spy there changeless beauty: still we feel thence ceaseless charm,
Drawing all the spirit from us, toward a home that knows no harm.

XXXVI.

Search the faith of all the nations: you shall find them by a sea,
Peering off from earthly sorrow, toward far lands of mystery;
Where, as firmly trusts each mortal, for the soul that does his best,
Gardens wait of endless plenty where an endless wish may rest.
All embark: the mists are heavy: down they fall, the skiffs between,
Dark-dividing every brother, shrouding every dearest mien:
Oh! but when all, all shall follow, shall not some cross o'er the main? —
Fann'd be hopes that brighten being! Heaven lures to naught in vain!

XXXVII.

Hard we strive for deeds immortal; but we die before our day:
And the soul that plann'd for manhood falls a child amid its play:
Deep we pant for rarer wisdom, higher views than Earth can give; —

Shall we never, never find them, where the wish fulfill'd may live?

XXXVIII.

Yes! I know of skeptic sages, and of proof that cannot pray;
That along the lines of feeling jars a contradictive "nay!"
"Gaze," say they, "and search about you: earth is green; and heaven is blue.
In the morn, before you knew it, calmly rose the sun to view.
Why should not the gentle vesper just as sóftly steal the day?
Come, while sunbeams strew the meadows, let us dance along the way;
Hunt the Fruit in arbors blushing; and be sure when sinks the eve
That our patient mother Nature shall these weary limbs receive,
And, as sweetly as she roused us on the dreamy morn of life,
Soothe exhausted powers to slumber, dead and consciousless of strife."

XXXIX.

Ah but Hope! can it be stifled? — Where that misty morn were you?
Did the mother's first caressing wake one joy to conscious view?
Whither then has fled the memory of that dear and doting voice?

Where the thought of those dull eyelids? where the
    the sight that fixt the choice? —
What was mind? — a dawning glimmer scarce in
    babe yet manifest.
What is mind? — it spurns to slumber, tho' the
    body faint for rest.
Down amid those grand reformers, see the elder
    leader swoon,
What is mind? — a life far stronger than in youth of
    blazing noon!
As the corpse the night frost withers, hark, the
    voice! it is not loud;
But the troubled nations tremble! sinks the soul
    within the shroud?

XL.

Trust me, mind is not like matter, moulded, weld-
    ed, multiple,
Numb in snow, and sprung in sunshine, by the
    storms dissoluble:
'Tis the breath of God! a spirit snared to work
    these lobes of clay:
'Tis the air that shakes the leaf, its home where'er
    a star can stray!

XLI.

Where was nature prone to wasting? or one power
    without its need?
Watch the brute, what fills his thinking? — mate,
    and young, and rest, and feed:
What the man's? — alas! you know it, how you
    tremble for the Fall:

How you tremble for the spirit, nor believe that
    death is all.
Oh, ye souls, who feel the future, meditate Eter-
    nity,
Doubt ye not that powers of being Nature's pur-
    pose verify! —

XLII.

Or that deeds — I saw a maiden track a thorny
    desert wide :
And I saw her face beam brighter, as she dash'd
    her tears aside :
On and on, tho' stumbling often, with a gaze in-
    tent she sped ;
While behind the path grew plainer from the blood
    her wounds had shed :
Then she fell, and, sweetly fainting, said : " My
    soul no more shall roam ! "
And, so smiling, left the body, which had borne
    her thus toward home !
Ah ! I felt that joy so real was a herald bright of
    Day,
At whose break, like mists at dawning, only darker
    life gives way.

XLIII.

Justice rules the course before us ! nay ! the
    throng'd fatigues and pains,
Which the patient martyr suffers, are not all that
    duty gains.
Sounding through the dying whispers of the men
    who live for God,

Throbs a call to grander life ere casting off expended sod.
Oh! I know, no whims in cloud are these bright towers beyond me spread:
And life's fickle prow I steady toward the beacons overhead.
All my love in them converging, what care I how strong the gale
Speeding time when, not a stranger, I shall reef my shatter'd sail!

XLIV.

If, too strain'd for earthly progress, age to weakness yield at length,
Without gain or power to forward, wherefore should I weep for strength?
From a solitary Patmos could the promise of the Lord
Still outvie a cherish'd mission, while one waited on His word:
After life below promotion lifts to rest of regions higher
With the Master-mind to witness how the Times attain desire.
And, still in the life below, Faith, Faith which is eternal gain,
Can outlive all disappointment, and make Wisdom's progress plain;
While the Beatific Vision bends to meet the reverent soul,
And the shades of partial living hie from dawning of the whole!

XLV.

Oh dawn thus, Thou Holy Spirit, Infinite, Unchanging Love,
Power, Truth, Wisdom, Justice, Beauty, throned eternally above;
Father of all works and worship; Father, Maker, Mover, Word,
Source, and Sum, and Destination, but apart from all, and Lord;
Life of ages, which, like echoes floating from eternity,
Spring through time to make Thy mandates mark'd to finite memory;
Life of spheres, where wandering wonders speak the praises of Thy dower,
Flash'd from seas of snowy summits, and instill'd above the flower;
Life of man, whose upright image, high-aspiring from the dust,
Looks to Thee, his pride, his pattern, his incitement, and his trust;
Life of life's unresting current, bearing all souls dream, or are,
Silent, swift, and broad, and blessed, toward eternal rest afar;
Thanks to Thee and adoration, that the mind, whose freedom hied
In the first strange dread of duty from the sway it had not tried,
Finds, 'mid rankest growth of doubting, naught to hide by human ill

Crystal touches of creation to reflect the Maker's will;
Wheresoe'er the danger threaten, that the lonely, trembling soul
Ne'er can tear itself from purpose destined for the general whole;
Or from Him, whose grandest glory all things are, and e'er shall be;
Or from Perfect Love, which governs wisely tho' with mystery.
Thanks, for Word of Inspiration, comfort, Christ, and Truth to prize;
And the golden fruit of ages ripening into Paradise!
And oh grant, All Conscious Spirit, — and the very prayer is bliss
Which can feel Thy nearing presence ere a word is formed of this, —
From the minds of those who seek Thee, and rely upon Thy might,
And on every loving token Thou has sent through all the night,
Lift away the veils of darkness, till each watchful eye may trace
Clearer, nearer to his vision, outlines of Thy destined grace;
Woo mankind to feelings kindly; rouse to deeds of charity;
Rid of lies, that soul to soul may grow an image bright of Thee.
Come at last, oh come, Lord Jesus, spreading worth from man to man;

Close the annals of confusion, draw the limits of
   the plan:
Quickly come, Oh Holy Spirit, sanctify the waiting
   world;
Burst the grander resurrection, from the earth beneath it whirl'd!
Call immortal life to regions, whence all sin and
   sorrow fall!
Raise, to reign in endless union with Thy Love!
   the All in All!

XLVI.

And for him whose watch still lengthens, whatso-
   e'er report be brought,
May he learn to wait, and doubt not of the glory
   to be wrought;
Thankful for all wish, and action, thought, or joy
   or misery,
Life, and every hope which lingers that the life
   may honor Thee.
Pardon him for ways that wander; and for words
   that are not wise,
And outweigh by contradiction all Thou canst not
   authorize.
Strengthen him, whate'er his fortune, ceasing never
   more to do,
But, in all his doing, trusting Thee alone to work
   the true.
Bide with him when danger deepens, proof against
   the final test,

Looking not to earth beneath him, but above, for all his rest,
Choosing, daring, doubting, learning, loving, serving, watching, then,
When shall come the great Deliverer, may he join the long Amen.

DO.

THERE came a time at which the poet's friends,
    Once more, from impulse swift of sudden joy,
Did meet with him. There, 'twixt the courses throng'd
Of praiseful scenes, he spoke:
                      "Peace, peace has come
For our loved land and cause, not less, I feel,
Than for the soul whose thought, these busy years,
Your kindness has found seasons to assist.
A weakness that has task'd your aid so long,
Dare it request one further service now?
A deed as dear to it as psalms of peace
To chief who dies 'mid dreams of work complete? —
I would intrust to you, dear friends, whate'er
Our mutual memories of life have gain'd.
Ah, we have found no Christ, only a man,
Weak, ignorant, bias'd, rash, ambitious, proud,
One prone to err, oft tempted from the right,
And yet train'd toward the good, as we may hope,
Because of pure Wish rear'd in a free land
Where only God's laws check development!
And if the tales do mirror forth true life,
From them, perchance, some may, as from true life, —
Told too through lips of a confiding friend, —
Trace wiser ways than man's; the mirror held
Not as a glass to children smiling still,
Fond of vain likeness, but as a kindred heart
Whose struggling life-throbs render likeness love,
Whose faults, tho' strong, train struggle, and, with it,
That one thing worthy here, a worthy Wish.
Yes, like the fount of Massah, moved by God,

I do believe that wish may spring t'revive,
Some germs that lurk e'en in the rock! flow thence
To make the barren desert bloom! all earth
A habitable home!
                " And you, dear friends,
You who have aided much, since all the truth
Seems half-truth without setting, will, perchance,
Add when how and by whom these tales were penn'd.
And if in aught Truth did bend modestly
To welcome in a mood inspiring it,
More whimsical with youth, more wise with age,
Truth, thus, may've gain'd in power to influence,
In form to make verse fitted for its aim —
To wake an inspiration through the world;
To rouse for music of a life complete
Some weary souls that turn aside from care,
'Mid restful musings on ideal good,
To read what pleases and may profit them.
God crown such aims! — and then, with growing worth,
Altho' these tales be told of one alone,
Their spirit shall speak life for more than one."

www.ingramcontent.com/pod-product-compliance
Lightning Source LLC
Chambersburg PA
CBHW031332230426
43670CB00006B/321